That We Might Have Joy

That We Might Have Joy

Desire,
Divinity &
Intimate Love

**Dr. Jennifer
Finlayson–Fife**

Faith
Matters

FM

FAITH MATTERS PUBLISHING
2929 W Navigator Drive, Suite 400
Meridian, ID 83642
faithmatters.org

ISBN: 978-1-953677-27-3 (paperback)

LIBRARY OF CONGRESS CONTROL NUMBER: 2025946439

POD*ed.* 10 9 8 7 6 5 4 3 2

To my mother, **GENIEL**,
who taught me to live
JOYFULLY.

To **JOHN**, with whom
I have shared so much
JOY.

Introduction:
The Disconnect
1

1

Eros:
The Spiritual Pursuit
of Communion
21

2

Deference & Denial:
Women's Struggle
with Desire
45

3

Shame & Suppression:
The Silent Struggle
of Men
73

4

Role-playing
in Marriage
93

5

Intimacy
Beyond Validation
119

6

Changing Our Minds
145

CONTENTS

7

Spiritual Development
& the Integration
of Sexuality
171

8

Discovering
the Soul of Sex
189

9

Toward an Embodied,
Sensual Faith
215

10

Ten Lessons
Toward a Child's
Sexual Integration
245

Appendix:
Making Sense of
Pornography
273

Acknowledgments
283

Endnotes
285

Further Reading
289

Colophon
291

Author
293

INTRODUCTION:
THE DISCONNECT

Nicole didn't realize just how seriously Grant was considering ending the marriage until the moment she found herself sitting across from me in my office. Over the years, Grant had made many attempts to address the difficulties in their relationship, but he hated upsetting Nicole—and nothing upset her more than talking about sex. So he was usually quick to retreat from the fraught conversations he started and quick to gloss over just how very frustrated he'd become.

Despite the difficulties with sex, there were in fact many good things about their marriage. In their thirty years together, they seldom fought and were respectful of each other in their shared efforts to educate their four kids and raise them in the church. For a long time, Grant coped with his unhappiness by focusing on the positive aspects of their relationship.

But when their youngest left for college, he found himself confronting a growing despair. In his view, he and his wife were something closer to coworkers than lovers, and he could no longer ignore just how isolated and hopeless he had become. As he sat on my couch next to his reluctant wife, he admitted for the first time the depth of his anguish and his doubts about whether he could continue to endure such a lonely marriage.

Attraction and affection had been a part of Grant and Nicole's courtship and early marriage. But once Nicole became pregnant with their first child, she lost the interest in sex she'd once felt. Nicole's greatest aspiration was to be a devoted mother, and in her mind, devoted motherhood was incompatible with being a woman who pursued or enjoyed pleasure—especially of a sexual nature. She knew this disappointed her husband, but it felt intuitively safer to distance herself from sex and what she saw as the baseness of it.

When it came to their sexual relationship, Nicole offered her husband polite affection in the day-to-day interactions of life and accommodated him sexually every month or so. For Nicole, a sexual marriage was not just intrusive, it was also counter to her understanding of a gospel-centered life. In her mind, spirituality was synonymous with obedience—and obedience meant restriction, self-control, and the avoidance of indulgent pleasures.

Nicole instinctively preferred a practical marriage, one centered on church participation and raising a family. She gravitated toward the belief that avoiding sex was morally superior to desiring it too much, and she often praised Grant for being better than the men who pressured their wives for it. Grant was more virtuous, she maintained, because he was willing to deny himself physical pleasure.

For the most part, this counter-pressure worked on Grant because he feared being seen (or seeing himself) as self-serving or worse yet—*carnal.* Eager to prove that he had indeed risen above "the natural man," Grant quietly (and resentfully) went along with their nearly sexless marriage. Beneath the surface, he harbored a quiet sense of superiority toward his wife, whose rigidity and anxiety was explicit. He liked to believe he was the stronger partner. But in reality, Grant struggled with his own fears around intimacy and sex. He too doubted himself and found it easier to conceal his desires than risk exposing them. Given their shared ambivalence about sexual intimacy and its place within a spiritual life, they instinctively created a superficially courteous and low-exposure relationship.

Grant and Nicole were devout members of the church—so much so that friends often referred to them as the anchors of their ward and stake. And in so many ways, they were. They accepted every calling extended to them and eagerly helped anyone in need. Because their marriage was also outwardly amiable and courteous, they looked the part of an ideal Latter-day Saint couple.

But beneath their picture-perfect exterior, the marriage was quietly unraveling. Although they appeared to epitomize spiritual strength, their marriage lacked depth and vitality. It offered them little to draw from—no sense of shared honesty, no sense of being truly known. Aside from their sparse sexual engagement, the marriage suffered from an overall lack of emotional freedom and ease in one another's presence. Grant and Nicole were so invested in their culturally validated identities that they feared knowing themselves, and each other, outside of them. A friendship that was *intimate* (as in open-hearted and honest) was not yet possible for this couple, and they each suffered because of it.

It was not the lack of sexual gratification that was eroding their happiness, it was the deep loneliness they felt in each other's presence. Like so many couples I work with, Grant and Nicole related to each other primarily through their respective responsibilities and roles. The safety and staleness of this orientation stifled the authenticity of their marriage, undermining the possibility of an intimate connection and honest passion.

Although marriage holds deep importance in The Church of Jesus Christ of Latter-day Saints, our instruction often emphasizes gender-based responsibilities and mutual respect more than principles that foster intimate marriages. Many of us were taught that a happy partnership rests on fulfilling our divine tasks: men are to lead, protect, and provide—both temporally and spiritually—while women are to nurture, rear, and support. The implicit message is that if each partner faithfully performs their respective duties, affection and marital harmony will naturally follow. But role fulfillment alone does not create an intimate marriage.

In fact, there are often tacit expectations about what one will get from a spouse in this implicitly dependent model. For example, it is common for young Latter-day Saint men to believe that sexual gratification will be the reward for faithfully providing for a wife and children. And many young women anticipate that a worthy priesthood holder will provide for them materially and spiritually, offering a parent-like protection in exchange for their dependence. So, when couples face the disconnect between their expectations and the lived reality of marriage, disillusionment and struggle often follow.

In no place is this disillusionment more conspicuous or more painful than in the unmet expectations around sex. Many of us assume that a strong sexual bond will naturally flow from the attraction that first drew a couple together. But for many religious couples, an inherited ambivalence toward sex and pleasure quietly undermines that outcome.

Though sexual expression is authorized within marriage, many Latter-day Saints continue to wrestle with the lingering belief that eroticism and spirituality are somehow at odds. We've long been taught that forsaking desire is a measure of goodness—that "putting off the natural man" is essential to righteousness. So, it is no wonder that pleasure within marriage can feel fraught: How much is too much? Under what conditions is it truly acceptable? Will sexual thoughts weaken the Spirit? For many, it's hard to trust themselves in intimacy when fear and abstinence have always been the answer.

I witness much of this confusion and pain in my work as a marriage therapist and educator. So many earnest LDS couples feel alienated from themselves and each other given their anxieties about the body and sexuality. Although we profess that sex in marriage is *good*, there is a significant disconnect between our teachings and our actual experiences, between our stated theology and our internalized beliefs. This lived dissonance compromises the quality of our marriages and the depth of our spirituality. If we are to be at peace, if we are to create loving, soulful partnerships, we must reconcile our sexual nature with our spiritual nature. We must find a way to be true to both.

To be clear, the struggle to feel at peace in our own bodies—and to view something as powerful and primal as sexuality with clarity and compassion—is a universal challenge, not one unique to Latter-day Saints. Yet, the way our theology is commonly (mis)understood leaves many of us unnecessarily estranged from our physical selves.

Even those who don't resonate with the level of sexual repression portrayed in Grant and Nicole's story may still operate within a narrow vision of what our sexuality and physicality can contribute to our spiritual lives. In reality, our theology offers us the possibility of a rich integration of body and spirit. If we want more *soul* in our relationships and greater joy in our lives, we must expand our understanding of our revealed faith to embrace the deep, life-giving truths available to us there.

REPRESSION DRIVES OBSESSION

Grant and Nicole's long-standing avoidance of their sexual relationship had clearly taken its toll. The pervasive loneliness and muted anger were testament to the fact that denying the sexual nature of marriage comes at a steep cost. When we treat sex as a lesser part of ourselves, we not only undermine our ability to create truly happy marriages, we also compromise a fundamental connection to ourselves.

Introduction: The Disconnect

The lack of intimate sex in Grant and Nicole's marriage was evidence of what the marriage had never become. The spark of attraction that once brought them together and fueled their early connection had long been snuffed by years of rigidity and unspoken fear. Their quiet resistance to deepening the intimacy of the marriage became a hidden wound—one that festered under the surface of their interactions and kept the relationship from thriving.

Unfortunately, Grant and Nicole's story is far from unique. In my private practice and workshops, I meet many faithful individuals who, like them, have bought into the idea that righteousness requires limiting one's relationship to sex. Their faith expresses a mindset where joy is peripheral, and the depth of human experience and connection is constrained by the fear of sin. Perhaps you have felt similarly—that sexuality and spirituality are incompatible bedfellows. As a friend of mine acknowledged candidly, "It is impossible for me to get in the mood when the Book of Mormon is on the nightstand."

Repression Drives Obsession

Equating spiritual strength with the denial of sexuality and pleasure is a common yet narrow understanding of our faith. The notion that the body is a hindrance to the soul runs deep across many religious traditions—we are not alone in our suspicion of the sensual. Yet this collective mistrust stands in stark contrast to the richness of our theology, which affirms that our bodies and sensual natures are not obstacles to holiness, but essential components of it.

While sexual self-mastery is indeed vital to spiritual wholeness, *self-denial* is not. In fact, when we reject our sexual nature and distance ourselves from the gift of the body, we create a spiritual fracture within. And paradoxically, our attempts at sexual *repression* are more likely to propel us towards sexual *obsession*, creating a spiritual turmoil that is precisely the opposite of what we are striving towards. In short, when we won't deal with our sexuality, it deals with us.

This was the case with Simon. Like many men I work with, he was tormented by his sexuality. In his early thirties and only a few years into marriage, he viewed pornography at intervals while simultaneously attending addiction recovery meetings. Yet in his concerted effort to put distance between himself and his sexual desires, Simon found they occupied even more of his mental and emotional space. His sexuality was an inescapable part of who he was, and his efforts to suppress his desires only deepened his despair and internal conflict. As much as he genuinely wished he could curtail these feelings—even excise them from his soul and psyche—his sexual behavior was increasingly a personal and marital preoccupation. 🕊️

Simon had grown up in a family focused on church attendance, scripture study, and obedience to the words of the prophet. His mother was anxious about sex, fearing that even learning about it might jeopardize her children's personal purity. She was quick to turn off the television whenever sexual references were made and was adamant that Simon's sisters dress modestly—bikinis were absolutely forbidden.

Although his parents were devout, they were not happily married, and Simon could track his mother's distress. Being a sensitive and intelligent boy, he tried to make his mother happy by getting good grades and living up to the expectations he learned at church. Simon was often praised for his earnestness, but in private, he felt lonely and distressed about the turmoil in his home. He kept this anxiety to himself, though, as his parents were too preoccupied with their own suffering to concern themselves much with his.

At age thirteen, Simon discovered online pornography. Not only were the forbidden images alluring, they provided him an escape into a pleasurable

🕊️ For a deeper exploration of my approach to pornography-related issues, see the appendix titled "Understanding Pornography."

(though deeply shameful) new world. His draw to the sexual depictions disrupted any view of himself as a good person, and he felt further pressured to hide the truth from his family and others who praised him for being a "righteous young man."

Without a way to understand his pull toward the erotic as anything other than personal and spiritual failure, Simon's obsession with pornography grew. He tried to manage his sexual thoughts with strategies like reciting scriptures and singing hymns, but terror at his own interest only seemed to intensify it. The harder he pushed his desires down, the more irresistible they became. Simon felt broken, but in the secrecy of his struggle, he eventually found a level of numbed comfort with porn that allowed him to view it off and on for years.

Simon held onto the hope that marriage would break him of his habit. Before marrying in his mid-twenties, he confessed to his fiancé Mary that he had struggled with porn "in the past." And for a time, while falling in love, the draw of porn indeed faded. Both he and Mary also assumed that the availability of sex in marriage would resolve the issue for good. This hope, however, proved misguided. While pregnant and nursing, Mary's desire for sex plummeted. And in Simon's frustration about the loss of his wife's attention, he turned to the familiar comfort of pornography—his private indulgence and quiet rebellion.

When Mary discovered that Simon was viewing porn, she resented both his choices and his dishonesty—but also felt somehow implicated by them. Raised to believe she was the steward of her husband's sexual needs, she couldn't help but feel she was failing him. Like many women I encounter, Mary saw her sexual availability as a way to keep her husband on the right path. But beneath her guilt was a deep disappointment that Simon had not lived up to the "good guy" persona he so comfortably projected. And in a tangle of conflicting emotions, she would make herself available for sex—hoping to curb his porn use—while simultaneously feeling repelled by it. She instinctively hated opening herself to someone she now saw as untrustworthy and self-indulgent.

In the wake of Mary's discovery, Simon resolved to attend the temple and study his scriptures with greater frequency. He felt a renewed determination to curtail his behavior and believed that deepening his spiritual devotion would be the antidote—the remedy to his unwelcome desires. But his earnest efforts did little to resolve the contradictory pulls within him. Even when he managed to avoid porn for weeks at a time, he could not find any sustained peace. Sexual fixation and shame were his constant companions—even during periods of "sobriety."

Simon's spiritual pursuits seem to be an intuitive solution in a culture that often pits sexuality against spirituality. Yet, our efforts to *eradicate* sexual feelings rather than *integrate* them amount to an act of self-rejection—one that inevitably leads to deeper fragmentation. Any spirituality that asks us to reject the body God gave us—including its capacity for pleasure—is a spirituality that is both suspect and fragile.

A more robust spirituality invites us to value the body and *integrate* our sexuality. This means we accept sexual desire and pleasure as valuable parts of life, while becoming agents—deliberate actors—within those feelings. When we have achieved *sexual integration*—a concept I will reference frequently throughout this book—we are capable of choosing from a place of integrity. This is to say, we are able to make conscience-driven choices that support our spiritual wellbeing and strengthen our most intimate relationships.

In contrast, if we repress (or indulge) sexual feelings reflexively, we remain governed by impulses—caught in spiritual turmoil around a core part of our humanity. In that internal dissonance, we cannot find ease in our bodies or trust in ourselves, which are both conditions essential for intimate sex and a soulful, embodied spirituality.

THE GOOD NEWS

Despite the fact that many of us feel fractured in our relationship to sexuality, we are blessed with a revealed theology that supports our sexual integration. Our faith teaches us that the body is not incidental to the soul, but essential to it. It also affirms that we are here to grow, and that we do this in

12

relationship. We can develop our capacity for intimacy and love most effectively in honest relationship with God and with one another. Loving connection offers us security and meaning in a difficult world. What's more, the ability to love and be loved, to know and be known, lies at the heart of spirituality and is the essence of Christianity: "And now abide faith, hope, love, these three; but the greatest of these is love." 🕮

One of the most powerful forms of love and intimacy draws on the spirituality of the body. Although we commonly think of the physical and sensual as counter to the spiritual, Latter-day doctrine supports the eternal truth that they are integrally connected. 🕮 Because the body is fundamental to the soul, sexuality can be a powerful pathway to the sacred. As Jeffrey Holland teaches, a "sexual union is . . . a very real sacrament of the highest order, a union not only of a man and a woman, but very much the union of that man and woman with God."[1] And as we will explore throughout this book, the gift of human intimacy deepens not only our connection to a spouse and divinity, it expands our capacity for joy.

While we can certainly relate to sexuality in ways that cause the *dis*-integration of our sexual and spiritual selves, this book explores how our faith

🕮 1 Corinthians 13:13 NKJV.

🕮 Doctrine & Covenants 93:33-34

13

invites us into the important soul work of integrating the two. The soul's longing to commune—with another, with God—encourages us to surrender our ego and our natural self-centeredness. And to the degree that we succeed in transcending our lesser selves for the higher aim of love and goodness, our sensual and moral capacities become more deeply aligned. In other words, as we grow—line upon line—in wisdom and love, we mature spiritually and relationally. We grow in our ability to know and love, and in this we become more capable of experiencing the sacred in sexual connection.

Facilitating this development in couples is at the heart of my work: I use the intimate terrain of marriage as a crucible for relational and spiritual growth. Intimacy—knowing and being known—pressures our development by revealing who we are. The exposures of marriage offer a valuable window into our character—character that often shows itself most clearly when we are not getting the approval or control we crave. How much truth—about ourselves and our relationship—are we willing to face and learn from? Can a couple create space for each other's gifts and honor their differences? Do spouses accept themselves and their God-given sexual nature enough to truly know and love one another through it? The answers to these questions reveal much about who we are, and where we must grow if we hope to become capable of intimate love in marriage.

WHAT LIES AHEAD

In the chapters that follow, we'll explore the relationship between sexuality and spirituality, and how marriage invites us to deepen and enrich that connection. To truly understand the spiritual nature of our sexuality, however, we must first examine some of the misconceptions that have taken root within our faith culture that keep us from our potential. In other words, it is essential to recognize what is false (yet often accepted as true) if we are to envision a spirituality that honors the body.

Some of the ideas we've inherited as doctrine are more accurately understood as *false traditions*—beliefs that keep us at odds with ourselves, distanced from God, and disconnected from the spiritual joy we are meant to know and experience within marriage. While we have received profound and inspired truths, many of us have also absorbed limiting and even harmful ideas. What we offer each other—no matter how well intentioned—can still mislead when it arises from a limited or mistaken point of view.

As moral agents by birthright, it is essential that we not be passive in discerning truth. We are called to "study these things out in our minds" and determine for ourselves what resonates with our spirits as truth. ☞ This sacred responsibility—to distinguish between right and wrong and then choose what is

☞ Doctrine & Covenants 9:7-9

15

right—is central to spiritual growth. My hope is that this book will support you in that endeavor, as you reflect on what you believe about the body and sexuality—and consider what fosters growth, peace, and a deeper connection with the sacred.

While it can be unsettling to challenge or dismantle familiar ways of thinking—especially before knowing what will take their place—it's important that we begin with an honest examination of the cultural beliefs that have limited our understanding of faith, the body, and sexuality. Not every reader will identify with all the specific ways these ideas have been interpreted or misapplied. Still, recognizing and understanding them is vital. At the very least, awareness can shed light on the messages many fellow Latter-day Saints have internalized and remind us of our shared responsibility not to perpetuate them.

In the first half of this book, we'll explore many of these inherited false traditions and how they subtly distort our relationship with ourselves and our sexuality—creating a kind of spiritual fracture. In the second half, we'll turn toward what's possible: I'll offer you a vision of the beauty and wholeness that can unfold when we make peace with the gift of our bodies and sexuality, and show you how our revealed faith points the way toward it. As I often tell my students, we cannot change what we cannot see.

So, this is how the chapters will progress: After establishing in chapter I that embodiment and sexuality are central to the gospel and essential to joy, chapters 2 and 3 examine the common yet unhelpful messages many Latter-day Saint women and men have received about gender and sexuality. Chapter 4 explores how these inherited ideas can conspire to undermine our marriages, creating low-intimacy and resentment-prone partnerships.

The second half of this book then explores how our faith points us to the integration of sexuality and spirituality: Chapters 5 through 7 examine how we grow in our capacity for love and intimacy through emotional and spiritual maturity. Chapters 8 and 9 delve more deeply into the relationship between sexuality, spirituality, and joy—with particular attention to intimate love in marriage. Finally, chapter 10 offers ten guiding principles for parents and teachers who wish to help children grow toward sexual integration.

The self-reflection questions at the close of each chapter are key to benefiting from the insights offered in this book. Reworking your relationship to sexuality and spirituality will likely require some reflection on your history, your relationships, and your inherited assumptions. Taking the time to write down your thoughts will help you clarify what these ideas mean for you personally. While sometimes cumbersome to write, this level of self-awareness is essential to making meaningful progress in this area of your life.

At its best, our theology fosters peace within our most intimate relationships and strengthens our faith in the goodness of God. Time and again, I've seen that as people come into deeper alignment with true principles, their sense of aliveness and inner freedom grows and their relationships improve. One woman recently shared with me:

> The principles you teach opened a door in my thinking that reshaped my whole world. For the first time, I could really see myself. (I had very little self-awareness before.) What I saw is that I had been cruel and unfair to my husband for years. I had controlled sex, taking hostage this gift meant to bless us and grow us. I told my husband (who I wasn't really friends with at the time) what I had learned about myself. I asked him to forgive me for being so self-focused and controlling. And I immediately changed what I could. The last three years we have had joy. The process is hard, and it's never done. But we are friends, we are lovers, and we are committed to growing ourselves and deepening our connection. Thank you for showing me how things could be. We found our way back to each other. We fell in love again. We changed our story. . . . Thank you for love.

At its heart, our theology points us to joy—and the gift of our sensual nature is deeply woven into that joy. I invite you to explore with me the life-giving and spiritual nature of sexuality: how it can enlarge our capacity for love and fortify our faith in the enduring goodness of God.

EROS: THE SPIRITUAL PURSUIT OF COMMUNION

Adam fell that men might be; and
men are, that they might have joy.

For Katie, falling in love with Eric was easy. Most of her friends had married years earlier, and she had begun to wonder whether she'd ever find someone to share her life with. Then, while visiting an out-of-town friend, she met Eric—and their connection was immediate and unmistakable. As their relationship deepened, Katie felt a kind of joy she had never experienced: the exhilaration of being fully seen and accepted filled her with new hope and excitement. She cherished every kiss and touch, even as the intensity of her desire sometimes unsettled her. And though she remained committed to her long-held belief in saving sex for marriage, her longing for Eric certainly tested that resolve in ways she hadn't anticipated.

Eighteen months prior to meeting Katie, Eric had lost his first wife to cancer. Katie understood that marrying Eric would mean uprooting her life—quitting her job, making a cross-country move, and taking on the role of stepmother to Eric's two young children. Despite the sacrifice, she was eager to do it. Katie was an altruist at heart, and the prospect of being useful in this way was instinctively appealing. Her own mother had been deeply self-sacrificing, pouring herself into the care of her husband and children—often at the cost of her own well-being. Though Katie could see that this total loss of self likely contributed to her mother's depression and emotional fragility, she knew of no other way to be a wife.

It wasn't long after the wedding that Katie felt a familiar heaviness creeping into her life. Caring for the children all day, then turning her attention to her husband's emotional and sexual needs in the evenings was the assumed and intuitive rhythm of their marriage. Yet, for Katie, it was soul-sucking. She wanted to be available to her husband, but as time went on, their intimate interactions felt increasingly invasive and overwhelming. Touching Eric was no longer an expression of desire. Instead, sex had become a duty to perform and an effort not to disappoint. Katie felt herself disappearing under the weight of obligation as a mother and wife and couldn't help but feel *used*. "If I never had sex again, it would be fine with me," Katie confessed when she first reached out to inquire about coming to see me.

The fading passion and dissolving happiness wasn't lost on Eric. Though he had a stronger desire for sex than Katie, her lack of enthusiasm made their intimate interactions less enjoyable for him as well. He longed for the sense of anticipation he felt in her touch when they were first falling in love. After suffering so much loss with the unexpected death of his first wife, Eric hadn't been sure if he would ever find happiness again. But then came Katie—beautiful and warmhearted as she was. He simply couldn't have been happier to find someone so wonderful to share his life with. Yet he watched as their early hope and excitement gradually gave way to the daily grind of work and parenting—and to a quiet, growing distance between them.

While Eric typically accepted Katie's unenthusiastic sexual accommodation, the implicit rejection felt humiliating in a way. He was being tolerated rather than welcomed, and their sexual relationship felt progressively more awkward—like they were *enacting* an intimate marriage more than *living* one. As much as he missed the passion in her touch, he was afraid to refuse the lifeless sex on offer. If he said no, would there be any hope of intimacy remaining in their marriage? Could he bear the loneliness that might follow? Katie and Eric couldn't understand how a relationship once filled with hope had become so burdened. How had they come to feel so distant when their relationship had been so promising in the beginning?

FALLEN, YET JOYLESS

Katie and Eric had experienced the transcendent gift of falling in love—the magnetism and hope in finding resonance with another soul. The strength of their attraction and their desire to be good to each other had given them every reason to hope for happiness. But as they began to share a life, and their insecurities and sexual differences came to the fore, they found themselves cast out of the garden of early love into a lone and dreary reality.

Every couple eventually encounters incompatibilities that disrupt the illusion of perfect harmony so often a part of early love. The way we respond to those differences shapes what the marriage will become. Most of us react in ways that undermine its intimacy and growth: We either push our spouse to do what we want, yield to their pressure for the same, or slip into an unwitting avoidance of the honesty that would expose these uncomfortable gaps. Our beliefs about who we should be—and how we should handle conflict—profoundly shape the depth and authenticity of a marriage.

The problem was that Katie and Eric had inherited ideas about marriage—from family and church—that emphasized keeping the peace but left little room for honesty. They believed a good marriage meant avoiding contention, which for them usually translated into sidestepping disagreement and withholding honesty when it might invite conflict and anger.

Katie, in particular, learned to suppress her own desires in order to keep the peace, focusing instead on meeting her husband's needs—just as she had seen her mother do. But this pattern of avoidance and self-denial, though well-intentioned, prevented the kind of honest, collaborative relationship that allows love to deepen. Rather than

24

creating a marriage that could thrive and sustain joy, they were quietly accumulating resentment and unmet expectations.

The truth is, while most of us long for closeness, we also fear the vulnerability and challenge of it—of being witnessed exactly as we are. We fear that if someone gets too close, they will either hurt us or discover something lacking and deem us unworthy. Just as often, we're afraid of losing ourselves in that closeness, unsure of who we'll be if we really let someone in.

Because these possibilities frighten us, most of us escape the exposures and demands of intimacy—both emotional and sexual—by focusing our time and energy on the safer tasks of work, church callings, and raising kids. Soon enough, though, we turn our marriages into something very different than they were at the beginning. What once felt alive with connection and possibility becomes something more predictable—safer, perhaps, but diminished in passion and joy.

We learn in the Book of Mormon that the goal of the spiritual project we are engaged in is *joy*: "Adam fell that men might be; and men are, that they might have joy." But even as we profess this understanding of God's larger purpose, joy so often eludes us. We either relate to it as a distant, theoretical promise—something to be granted in the next life—or we live (much like Katie did) as though our

2 Nephi 2:25

obedient long-suffering is God's true aim. In fact, many of us view joy as almost *suspect* in a person committed to faith—as if true devotion is expressed through self-denial.

How should we understand our theology of joy? If, as scripture teaches, joy is the purpose of our creation, how does the gospel guide us toward it?

Suffering is an inescapable part of life, even when we've made the best possible choices. It follows that joy cannot depend on the absence of sorrow and loss. Instead, joy seems to arise from a kind of generosity towards life—an openness to life's lessons, the willingness to trust rather than retreat, to love when self-protection would seem safer. This generous disposition is an expression of faith, and it opens us to receiving the goodness and beauty that is a part of joy.

Joy is also deeply tied to the quality of our relationships. As we'll explore, living our Christianity means courageously reaching beyond ourselves and truly caring about others, and in so doing we create the interpersonal connections our souls need. Rich friendships—deep, honest bonds—are not just comforts; they are central to joy. In fact, research consistently affirms that close, meaningful relationships both in and outside marriage are the most powerful predictor of emotional wellbeing and life satisfaction. ☞

☞ A major longitudinal study on health and wellbeing found that close, meaningful relationships are the single most powerful predictor of joy—far outweighing wealth, status, or achievement.[1]

26

Indeed, building rich, honest marriages seems to be essential to God's larger project, but "joyless" might have been the best way to describe Eric and Katie's sexual relationship. Facing Katie's rejection was painful for Eric, so his initial goal in our work together was fewer refusals, hoping to increase the frequency of the bad sex they were having. Yet, the greatest challenge to their happiness was not the frequency of their encounters, it was the loss of attraction and delight with one another. Eric and Katie, like so many couples, wanted to feel alive in each other's arms again, and increasing the amount of routine sex was not going to address the root of their problem.

Whether we like it or not, mutual desire plays a crucial role in the happiness of partnerships. When research participants were recently surveyed about the qualities in marriage that were most important to them, "love and passion" topped the list.[2] As President Spencer W. Kimball once said and as research backs up, the absence of reciprocal desire erodes marital happiness and is a significant contributor to divorce.[3] As much as we may want to believe that mutual enjoyment is only the frosting in a viable, joyful marriage, it is, in reality, the cake.

Why is this the case when marriage offers so many benefits beyond sex and desire? Why does shared pleasure in each other matter so deeply to a couple's overall happiness? Whether or not we believe we should, most of us long to feel chosen—to be seen as special by our spouse. This is what we experience when we first fall in love, and what we hope to keep feeling together. It is the soul-deep pleasure of *eros love*—to be known and desired *as we are*.

What is eros love? Eros is one of four types of love in Greek philosophy (the others being *philia*, *agape*, and *storge*), and it is linked to romantic love and sexuality. Although eros is the root of eroticism, it is much more than sexual love. To the Greeks, eros was seen as *the life force*—the energy that binds us to the world. It draws us into connection—with mystery, with virtue, with one another. Eros unsettles our complacency and calls us into unfamiliar terrain—it is the human yearning to become something more.

As human beings, we long for love and knowledge—for what we do not yet have and what we do not yet know. And the willingness to step beyond our immediate comfort—to change, to create, to love—is at its core an expression of faith. It is the embodiment of hope. When we live this kind of faith, we grow into more loving and able people. And in this generativity, we're filled with a deep sense of meaning and vitality.

Eros should not be confused with hedonism or the indulgent pursuit of pleasure. A red-light district, for example, represents anything but the erotic. Sex is everywhere, and yet, such places are full of its opposite energy: *thanatos*. Thanatos is *the death instinct*, according to the Greeks. It is despair,

28

disconnection, and the refusal to grow. Thanatos resists change and shrinks from the vulnerability that intimacy requires. It is the voice of ego—craving comfort and control. While eros reaches outward in pursuit of connection, thanatos retreats inward, seeking the illusion of invulnerability.

While the eros call to grow beyond ourselves can be expressed in any domain of life, the erotic invitation to transcend ourselves happens most powerfully in intimate love. Theologian C. S. Lewis and psychologist Carl Jung describe the essence of eros love as the human desire *to be with* another soul—another self—and to know them in every way. To fall in love is to experience this kind of communion—an awakening that lifts us out of our insular reality into magnetic connection with another. *It happens to us*, and that mix of exhilaration and vulnerability transforms our experience of ourselves and the world.

But to love a romantic partner over the long term requires us to become more than we currently are. We must make room for them in our hearts and lives; we must operate outside of our self-interest on their behalf. To love a marriage partner erotically asks us to grow into someone capable of caring for another person, body and soul.

While we have come to associate the word *eroticism* with pornography and commercialized expressions of sex, these are perversions of what constitutes the erotic. The erotic is life-giving, rooted *primarily* in our longing for intimacy and deep connection. It is *secondarily* the desire to be sexual with that captivating other—to share our whole selves with them and to commune with them sexually, too.

This is captured beautifully in a line from the film *About a Boy*, when a young adolescent tries to make sense of his love-sick attraction and expresses how his feelings transcend mere sex. He says: "I want to be with her. I want to be with her all the time. I want to tell her things that I don't want to tell you or Mum. I suppose if I could have all those things, *I wouldn't really mind if I touched her*." This is the essence of eros love.

While many couples may not have language for this desire, those in stagnant marriages are often yearning for something more heartfelt and alive. Most of us long to feel special to each other, to know we are seen and accepted. We want the spark of life that eros love brings to marriage—both in how we are friends and how we are lovers.

Erotic marriages are less something we fall into and more something we intentionally cultivate. We create a deeper sense of aliveness when we bring our best to one another—when we keep the marriage truthful, dealing honestly with differences, and safeguarding the relationship from outside interference. Even if a marriage feels dormant, its spark can be rekindled through a shared commitment to growth. How truthful and invested we are, how free we are to be ourselves and make room for the other, has everything to do with eros desire.

Modern research supports the fact that there are many benefits to frequent, positive-meaning sex, including fewer sick days, stronger immune and cardiovascular systems, slower aging, and less physical pain.[4] Beyond the many health benefits, there is a strong correlation between mutuality in sex and marital happiness.[5] Couples who create a fulfilling sexual relationship are not only more likely to stay together, their sexual bond makes them more resilient when they are confronted with stressors both inside and outside the marriage.[6]

Eros: The Spiritual Pursuit of Communion

What is it about sexual intimacy that makes couples happier in marriage? The physical pleasures of sex indeed contribute to our wellbeing. Oxytocin (a hormone released after orgasm) increases feelings of trust and attachment to a spouse. However, when it comes to the quality of a couples' relationship, the affirmation of desire for one another that sex expresses is more important than simply shared physical pleasure: You are the one I desire; you are the one I find compelling to touch; I value *you*—this is the meaning we seek. This is the energy that separates an intimate relationship from every other. And this sense of being desired, *chosen*, and cherished, is what matters to us most in erotic love.

In other words, the loss of ardency or spark in our partner's gaze may undermine marital happiness even more than the infrequency of sex. Mutual attraction and desire is far more valuable in bonding a couple than is going through the motions of sex. Psychologist and researcher John Gottman defines this honest mutual validation as "fondness and admiration," and his research shows that couples' enthusiasm for the other is fundamental to romance, passion, and the resiliency of a partnership.[7]

Also, the embodied expressions of eros in sex powerfully bind us to one another. When the sexual expresses the erotic—the desire for another soul—it can be a deep source of not just wellbeing but spirituality, too. As apostle Parley P. Pratt expressed:

> Some persons have supposed that our natural affections were the result of a fallen and corrupt nature, and that they are "carnal, sensual, and devilish," and therefore ought to be resisted, subdued, or overcome . . . ; Our natural affections are planted in us by the Spirit of God for a wise purpose; . . . they are the very main-springs of life and happiness— they are the cement of all virtuous and heavenly society—they are the essence of charity or love.[8]

While erotic love is divine in origin and powerful in deeply bonding a couple, many of us are not capable of freely offering sexual love because we are ill at ease with ourselves and our sexual natures. In our earnest efforts to be good, many of us focus our spirituality on self-denial, and cut ourselves off from the blessing of our sensuality. Anxieties about the body, intimacy, and pleasure keep many of us from an important element of spirituality and joy—"the main-spring of life and happiness"—that our souls need.

CARNAL, SENSUAL, & DEVILISH

During the evening party following our temple sealing, friends, family, and members of the ward waited in a long, formal reception line to wish us well, leave a gift, and enjoy some wedding cake before heading home. We loved our wedding day and were supported by so many good people who cared about us and wanted our success.

But our traditional LDS celebration stood in stark contrast to the Jewish wedding we attended a month later. Shortly after our friends spoke their vows beneath the chuppah and broke the ceremonial glass, the wedding guests interlocked arms, encircled the newlyweds, and held them up on chairs overhead. As family and friends danced the traditional hora around the bride and groom, we expressed through our bodies the meaning of the moment: A couple had promised under God to love each other, as their family and friends encircled, supported, and celebrated them. Our physical participation in this collective meaning underscored the beauty and meaning of their vows in a way that stiff reception lines could never express or adequately celebrate.

In contrast to the embodied joy we experienced at the Jewish wedding, I remember as an adolescent observing rigid, slightly awkward adults dancing at the Gold and Green Ball, an annual stake dance. Granted, without the assistance of alcohol, it takes courage for any self-aware adult to mimic a rhythm and move unscripted while others look on. Still, I could instinctively sense the collective effort to keep ourselves from feeling too much or moving too freely. We managed to dance without letting our sensuality enter the experience—to move without letting the body lead. Any surrender to feeling might threaten our grasp on virtue and risk exposing, to others and even ourselves, the reality of our sexual nature.

Despite a theology that recognizes the importance of the body to our spirituality, as Latter-day Saints we work very hard to stay above the neck. We like the safety of ideas and discussion, of logic and formality. This is how we worship. If we keep our bodies out of our religious practices and celebrations, perhaps we'll remain rational enough to fend off sensual abandon or the vulnerability of unguarded feeling.

This subtle but real collective alienation from our bodies is perhaps most evident at my women's retreats. While we learn in church that our bodies are divine in nature, most of us, even if subconsciously, consider our genitals and our capacity for pleasure to be a lesser part of ourselves. The body is good—*except for the bad parts*. Even looking at an anatomical drawing of the vulva during an instructional session requires an extra dose of courage for many of the participants. Resisting that instinctive self-rejection, I teach participants all about this amazing structure, including how the sole function of the clitoris is to impart pleasure to its owner. Unlike the penis, which serves multiple functions, the clitoris takes care of no one but the woman herself—a telling design indeed.

I also teach the participants how important acceptance of our bodies is to loving and being loved in marriage, to intimately knowing and being known. If you cannot be at peace with your sexual self, can you really let a spouse in on who you are? Can you expect a spouse to accept what you reject? These are often challenging and reorienting questions for retreat participants.

Beyond instruction about our sexual anatomy, I teach women that we must receive and celebrate our feminine bodies if we are to truly access our strength. This kind of self-acceptance is not indulgent—it's foundational to becoming capable of sexual intimacy. To integrate our sexuality is to make peace with our embodied selves and be an agent within that sensual and sexual capacity. Without this integration, we remain a "house divided"—alienated from ourselves, always in a state of self-distrust.

To this end, I share video clips of traditional cultural dances with attendees: Polynesian women jubilantly shaking their tail feathers and undulating their spines, Italian women dancing the Pizzica. These traditional dances express an integrated femininity—a cultural acknowledgment of women's sensuality that enables them to simultaneously claim their sexuality *and* their dignity. This expression of sexuality doesn't flaunt, nor does it apologize.

Carnal, Sensual, & Devilish

Instead, these cultural dances offer a way for women (and men) to be joyful in their bodies—to assimilate through dance an embodied femininity (and masculinity) into their sense of who they are.

After watching several cultural variations of traditional feminine dance, we end the day with an exercise class full of hip circles and pelvic tilts that imitate early fertility dances. What often starts as self-consciousness and nervous laughter eventually gives way to genuine delight. I watch as women begin connecting to a long-dormant part of themselves—a part they may not have known was missing, or believed they shouldn't acknowledge. But in discovering and experiencing it, they awaken to feel full of life and less apologetic for who they are. They begin to radiate soul beauty and joy as they connect to eros. It's a remarkable thing to witness.

After returning from a recent women's retreat, a participant, Miriam, wrote to me:

> Something unlocked and opened inside of me. When I got home, it was like fireworks! My husband and I connected on such an intimate level. And I guess everything was just right because after

ten years of unexplained infertility, and finally giving up on the prospect of a biological child of our own, I just found out today I am pregnant! I had to take the test twice because I couldn't believe it! I just had to write ... and let you know how appreciative I am! My husband says [the principles] you [taught] unlocked me! ... Thank you for a retreat I'll never forget.

THE SPIRITUALITY OF SEX

Contrary to what we may fear, it is not our bodies that divide us from God and wisdom. In fact, our ability to feel and act is critical to our spiritual perception and progression. While many faith traditions treat the body as a threat to the spiritual, Latter-day Saints understand embodiment as central to it. Christian asceticism, for example, renounces all sensual pleasure in an effort to achieve a higher spiritual state. But our theology recognizes spiritual growth as integrally tied to the body.

We believe that a body is necessary for the spiritual aim of becoming more like our Parents in Heaven. Beyond sharing a physical likeness, embodiment is critical to our soul's progression and becoming as They are. Apostle James Talmage articulated our theology well: "[We] look upon these bodies of ours as gifts from God. We Latter-day Saints do not regard the body as something

37

to be condemned, something to be abhorred. . . . We regard the body as the sign of our royal birth-right. . . . It is peculiar to the theology of the Latter-day Saints that we regard [the body] as an essential part of the soul."[9]

To underscore this last point, we understand that "the spirit *and* the body are the soul of man,"👉 which is to say that the body is *integral* to the soul, and not just a vessel for it. As we'll explore in the pages ahead, this definition of the soul is key to understanding the intrinsic connection between our sexuality and our spirituality. One will always shape and inform the other, and it is not possible to neglect one and thrive in the other.

Some people perceive our restrictions on sex outside of marriage as a rejection of sex, as proof that sex is a lesser part of us that needs the con-tainer of marriage to neutralize it. We would do better to consider the expectation of commitment as an effort to protect our souls. Chastity, properly understood, is a way of exercising care toward our sexuality.[10] In saving sex for marriage, for a context of love and commitment, we are striving to elevate sex to something capable of bringing us solace and joy—something capable of giving us anchor in a turbulent world.

Sex, of course, is not *inherently* good. When used exploitatively, in marriage or not, it is deeply destructive. But sex *can* be good, even very good.

👉 Doctrine & Covenants 88:15; emphasis added.

38

And at its best, it expresses our love and enjoyment of one another. It can be a way to celebrate our lives and love, and this kind of sex is very good for our souls. By elevating the meaning of an intimate relationship through *who we are* and *what we choose*, we can find sanctification in sex—soul-sustenance even—through the beauty we create there.

This capacity for soulful sex is proportional to our capacity for love and intimacy. In other words, the ability for sex to be sanctifying and spiritually anchoring is dependent upon our ability to know and love another through it. Few of us are as good at this as we want to believe. In fact, the exposures of marriage readily reveal how easily we self-serve in the name of love—how quickly we critique a spouse for their failures towards us instead of attending to our own deficiencies in love. How resistant we are to being seen as we truly are, in sex and in life. Yet, the container and crucible of marriage is what helps us learn to love.

Marriage can deepen our ability to love, including our ability to love erotically. This doesn't happen without effort. It requires our commitment to a soul-stretching process that includes the courage to see ourselves truthfully. It means resisting the urge to hide, to punish, or to retreat when disappointment arises—whether in ourselves or in our partner. As my son said when he was nine, "The reason you need a wife is to tell you if you have ticks or moles on your back." (Truth from the mouths of babes!) A spouse sees what we don't—no one knows our lesser selves, our private failures, and self-deceptions—better than a spouse. Nothing reveals us to ourselves as quickly as a disillusioned partner. This is what intimacy is.

We want to believe that intimacy feels good, and sometimes it does. But more often intimacy exposes us and pushes us to see the unflattering aspects of who we are—the places we must grow to become capable of love. Intimacy's raw exposures can be uncomfortable, even painful, but they are precisely what drive our growth. They are, in fact, the gifts we need. It is through learning to love in the face of those disappointments and disillusionments (in ourselves or our partner) that we become more than we are. This is to choose erotically.

When I work with clients, my goal is to surface the truths a couple needs in order to grow—truths that they have been intuitively avoiding. I try to pull back the veil on what the couple is living but has resisted acknowledging. Most of us fear that the truth will only make things worse. We fear the disorientation that usually comes with allowing into our awareness realities we don't yet know how to respond to. So, we resist the truth instead—the truth we need to evolve and keep a marriage alive.

After coming to me for help, Katie and Eric were dutifully doing the exercises I'd given to them—practices designed to help them create a richer embodied connection, and a technique to help Katie experience orgasm for the first time. Yet, every week Katie came back discouraged. "Nothing's working," she would say. Though she wanted Eric to not be displeased with her, her own desire was elusive, and she wasn't sure anything would change that.

This was hard for Eric to take in. He loved Katie and wanted her to desire him. So, he imagined that if he just tried harder, he could somehow resolve her low desire. He was sincere in his efforts—diligently following the assigned exercises and learning the techniques that might stimulate her best. But to Katie, all of Eric's efforts were just more pressure. "I'm afraid I'm just fundamentally broken," she confessed at one meeting.

After several meetings with little progress, I shared with Katie what I could see in her:

"You're approaching the exercises much like you approach sex—*dutifully*, but without much heart. You want Eric to see that you're making an effort, but it's not clear to me that you truly want this. I'm confident your sexual relationship could really improve, but only if it's something you desire. Right now, it feels like you're going through the motions as a way to avoid confronting your own uncertainty—whether a meaningful sexual relationship with Eric is something you desire or not."

To be fair, Katie *truly* didn't like sex. She recoiled from every touch, trying to protect herself from exposure and the sense of being taken from. Eric was not a taker, but she had watched her mother fold into her father's life, and she anticipated losing herself even more in sex. As long as Eric was in pursuit, she could accommodate him while avoiding the exposure of real investment in an intimate relationship. In accommodating, Katie was also avoiding the risk of really choosing who she wanted to be—choosing either to create an intimate sexual relationship with Eric or explicitly choosing not to.

To Eric, I said: "Maybe it's time to face what your wife is saying to you implicitly—that she would prefer to accommodate you on occasion, and tell herself she's done her part—than create something mutual with you. She either cannot or does not want to offer something more. So, more effort on your part is not going to get Katie to want what you want. In fact, the more you push, the more she either resentfully accommodates or resists you. Desire doesn't grow through pressure—it grows when both people are free to choose, and I believe Katie is quietly asserting a choice."

These kinds of intimate exposures—when we see our limitations or recognize our part in our unhappiness—often disrupt our sense of reality and unsettle the equilibrium with ourselves or our partner. But the deeper accommodation of truth invites us into choices more congruent with who we desire to be and what we can genuinely respect within our circumstances.

The phrase "the truth shall set you free" carries deep wisdom, but the truth often wounds before it heals. It wounds our egos and shatters our self-deceptions even as it liberates, giving us the ability to make wiser, more compassionate choices. This is

42

the potential for growth that the inherent intimacy of marriage offers us if we can receive it. It will certainly test our faith.

In these moments of truth, we have a choice between faith and fear, between eros expansion and thanatos retreat. We can demand that our relationships yield to reality as we know it, or we can step into the uncertainty that love and growth asks of us. Faith—the courage to do what we know is right—is the only way we create a deeper coherence within ourselves and deeper integrity within our relationships.

You'll hear more about Katie and Eric's story in chapter 6, but in brief, they each choose faith. By stepping beyond the selves they knew and the control they were instinctively seeking, they grew into people more capable of knowing each other, and more capable of love. In their deepening integrity, they forged the ability to be truer friends and more honest lovers. More invested in each other, and at the same time, more free.

This kind of development is what makes a marriage feel alive again. It is what makes us free to be ourselves while being simultaneously deeply committed to another. Because as a couple accommodates more truth, the marriage has more life and light in it. The eros energy that is a part of this growth usually leads couples to experience richer connection and genuine attraction. It is what makes sex truly erotic.

In his talk, "of Souls, Symbols, and Sacraments," Jeffrey Holland teaches that loving sexuality in marriage can be a merger of "mortals and deity," and that intimate sex allows us to participate in a sacred energy. It is through our bodies that we access this sacred energy and receive the solace and sanctification we need.

To become capable of this kind of communion, we must first recognize and surrender some of the false traditions we have absorbed and even clung to. In the next three chapters, we will explore some of these misconceptions about marriage, sexuality, and spirituality that often stand in our way as we seek to increase our capacity for intimacy and our potential for joy.

DEFERENCE & DENIAL: WOMEN'S STRUGGLE WITH DESIRE

"Who can find a virtuous woman?
for her price is far above rubies."
—*Proverbs 31:10*

Rachel had always been a keen observer of others, attuned to the unspoken dynamics around her. Even as a young girl, she noticed the fractures in her parents' marriage. She sensed her mother's unhappiness—the toll that childrearing and keeping the household afloat took on her. She also felt the quiet disapproval her father harbored toward her mother—his judgment and discontentment rippled through their home.

Not only was Rachel sensitive to the challenges in her parents' marriage, she was herself conscientious and earnest. She wanted to be good, believing that if she were obedient and helpful enough, she might ease some of her mother's burden. She also longed to become the kind of girl a future husband would love.

So, when she heard at church that the most righteous girls set aside personal ambitions for the sacred roles of wife and mother, Rachel took it to heart. Righteous women, she was taught, served selflessly and cheerfully—without complaint and without the expectation of external accolades. These ideals, combined with her natural sensitivity, came to deeply shape Rachel's understanding of who she was supposed to be.

Rachel's inclination to accommodate others became second nature. She rarely expressed or even allowed herself to fully recognize her own desires—especially if they conflicted with someone else's. For instance, when her mother bought her clothing that reflected her mother's taste—sporty and practical—rather than the more feminine styles that Rachel preferred, Rachel didn't complain. She felt guilty registering a wish that might add to her mother's stress.

As Rachel entered the Young Women program, the messages continued: the virtue of sacrifice, the sacred roles of wife and mother, and the importance of sustaining a future husband in his priesthood responsibilities. But perhaps most formative were the lessons that linked a woman's worth to her sexual purity. To be "morally clean"—untouched by sexual sin—was not just a virtue but an important measure of desirability. Hoping to be chosen by a worthy young man, she resolved to push aside these emerging feelings.

When Rachel met Dan several years later, they fell in love quickly and married in the temple within the year. Having absorbed the message that a career wasn't really compatible with the higher callings of wife and mother, Rachel cut short her training as a dental hygienist to start a family. It wasn't the decision to stay home or have children that left Rachel in a vulnerable position—many women choose this path out of their own desires and sense of agency. The issue was that for Rachel it wasn't really a choice. She believed this was the *only* acceptable option for her. And because she needed so much for others to see her as "good," her embrace of the prescribed path wasn't an act of personal conviction so much as an effort to earn the approval of others—church members, her family, and even God. She didn't consider a different path; in fact, she didn't even allow herself the space to imagine one. For Rachel, obedience and external validation were strong motivating forces behind her choices.

But nineteen years and six children into marriage, Rachel felt as though she were disappearing in her own life. Her husband had recently been called to be the bishop of their ward, and this required her to do even more of the childrearing in isolation. She was used to managing many of these demands on her own, but now Dan was gone most Sundays and several evenings each week while she put in untold hours of thankless, behind-the-scenes work. "Your husband is just amazing!" ward members would often tell her; "He does so much for everyone."

Dan was praised not only for his church service but also for his success as a physician. And while Rachel appreciated the comforts his achievements provided, she couldn't shake a quiet sense of inferiority—rooted, in part, in her financial and emotional dependence on him.

Although he assured her that he respected and loved her, there seemed to be an unspoken understanding between them that she was there to support *his* life.

Though she disliked feeling a step down from Dan, she was accustomed to self-doubt. In fact, her own beliefs and desires were not very clear to her most of the time. Dan, on the other hand, was very opinionated and even condescending at times. When Rachel sometimes voiced her frustrations about his dismissiveness, Dan would make an effort to take her perspectives and desires more seriously. But in the end, it was usually Dan's judgment that prevailed. Rachel, prone to second-guessing herself and drawn to the reassurance of Dan's apparent certainty, slipped easily into a dynamic where his preferences quietly took the lead.

Because Dan appeared to be the steadier of the two, Rachel leaned on him for reassurance and a sense of mattering. But offering that kind of emotional support wasn't something he did well. He felt the pressure to make his wife happy, and yet making Rachel happy never really worked. She was anxious and empty much of the time, and Dan was often frustrated by her self-doubt and needy disposition.

Being insecure himself and needing to see himself as stronger than his wife to feel like a man (a message *he* had internalized), he never sincerely challenged Rachel's inclination to defer to him. He had no vision of a *collaborative marriage*—no real understanding of how a couple might contribute their differing perspectives and gifts as equals towards a shared goal.

It is perhaps no surprise that Rachel struggled with sexual desire. Although Dan often told her that she was beautiful, these reassurances most frequently surfaced when he wanted to have sex. His compliments were indeed genuine, but she didn't *feel* desirable. While it was clear that Dan desired sex, it wasn't obvious to Rachel that he desired *her*. And that distinction mattered. Rachel knew she mattered to Dan—she filled an important role in his life—but it wasn't clear that he genuinely liked her for herself. And the truth was, Rachel wasn't entirely sure who that was. Uncertain of her own identity, she couldn't imagine she could be truly compelling to anyone.

So she did what her mother told her the night before her wedding: "Have sex when he asks and take care of his needs." This approach made sense to her in a way—Rachel liked being needed by Dan and accommodating him sexually was one way to do this. But it also served another purpose—it made sex less intimate. By approaching sex as a marital duty, Rachel could avoid exposing her eroticism and even her heart. It gave her a way to shield herself from the doubts that gnawed at her—the questions she harbored about the depth of Dan's love and desire for her.

Although Rachel found some safety in this approach to sex, it also left her unsettled. The truth was that Dan seemed to always get what he wanted. And the more she gave, the more it felt like she faded into the background—unseen and unacknowledged by the very person she was giving so much to. In time, this left her feeling used and resentful, turning sex into something she largely endured. She was puzzled by women who claimed to enjoy it—how could that be? For her, the whole experience felt more like a chore, something to get through rather than enjoy.

Instead of confronting the growing disconnects and unanswered questions in her marriage, Rachel poured herself into motherhood—a role that felt far more certain and enjoyable. She channeled her energy into her children's lives, finding real joy in their growth and accomplishments. Her children loved and relied on her, and this not only felt good, it gave her a deep sense of purpose. The marriage, while not very intimate, functioned well enough to raise a family. It simply lacked the closeness and attraction that Rachel had once anticipated in marrying Dan.

Rachel's approach to marriage is one that is common among my female clients: women devote themselves almost entirely to parenting and church service, with little connection to an identity beyond these roles. They value their husbands as providers and spiritual leaders, but the emotional and sexual intimacy in the marriage is limited. For many, sex is approached as a duty—a marital responsibility—rather than an expression of desire or a reflection of their investment and pleasure in the relationship.

While church messages about women's roles have expanded somewhat in recent years, many

LDS women still find themselves shaped by a culture that emphasizes obedience to prescribed gender roles over the deeper spiritual work of becoming whole—of cultivating and offering their distinct gifts to the world.

It matters what our spiritual objectives are because they significantly influence who we become. Most of us look to the communities we belong to (family, church, and the larger society) for cues about what it means to be virtuous, what it takes to succeed, and what is possible for us as men and women.

As we'll explore in chapter 6, we need expectations and cultural standards. They offer structure and guidance as we begin the work of forging a sense of self early in life. But if they are too rigid or exacting, if they pressure excessive conformity, they can actually interfere with our ability to grow into *individuals*—into the creatures we were meant to be. As Christ said in the Gospel of Thomas, "If you bring forth what is within you, what is within you will save you. If you do not bring forth what is within you, what you do not bring forth will destroy you." ☞

In other words, fulfilling the measure of our creation not only allows us to contribute to the body of Christ—to the collective of the church and humanity—we also forge a peace with ourselves as

☞ The Gospel of Thomas is a non-canonical collection of sayings attributed to Jesus, part of the Nag Hammadi library discovered in Egypt in 1945.

51

we develop and share who we are. This requires a broader view of what it means to do God's will—one where the highest moral values extend beyond rigid gender scripts or narrow notions of obedience.

As we'll see in this chapter and the next, our inherited ideas about gender and sexuality, while often helpful as a starting point, can just as easily hinder our ability to know ourselves, make authentic choices, and create truly intimate marriages. What follows are some of the meanings around womanhood and sex that clients and research participants received that measurably limited their ability to be at peace with themselves, to integrate their sexuality and to create intimate marriages.

"BECAUSE YOU ARE A WOMAN": MESSAGES OF IDEAL FEMININITY

Despite recent shifts in lesson manuals and temple ceremonies towards greater equality, most adult Latter-day Saint women have been raised in a tradition that taught them to look to and depend on men. Because priesthood authority is conferred upon men, they are positioned to preside over meetings, families, and even marriages. Rachel understood this to mean that her voice carried slightly less weight in their shared decisions, since her husband—through his priesthood—was presumed to have greater access to truth. Beyond that, Rachel had internalized the idea that she *should* suppress her own preferences and desires whenever they conflict with her responsibility to support her husband as the spiritual and temporal leader of their home.

Rachel—like many Latter-day Saint women—learned that the ideal woman willingly sets aside personal aspirations to care for her husband and children. While motherhood is unquestionably a sacred and meaningful vocation, for many women, this framing meant that desiring anything beyond it was selfish, or even a sign of spiritual weakness. As a thirty-something workshop participant recently said to me: "I don't even know how I learned it, but I've always known my job is to be a support for my husband and kids."

Deference & Denial: Women's Struggle with Desire

My client Audrey did not pursue a college degree and instead married when she was twenty years old. Shortly after the birth of their fourth child, Audrey's husband admitted he had developed a close connection with a female colleague—and that one evening, after work, they had shared a kiss. Understandably, the revelation sent Audrey and their marriage into crisis.

Disillusioned and insecure, Audrey found herself reckoning with the vulnerability of the position she had put herself in. If the marriage unraveled—if he left—she lacked the means to adequately support herself. In earnestly following what she believed was God's will, she had entrusted her future to a man who was proving less trustworthy than she had once believed. Having married so young, she now saw how little she'd understood her own desires when she made choices that would shape the rest of her life.

In our conversations, Audrey spoke of the many messages she received as an adolescent that encouraged her toward the dependent path she chose. She referenced a conference talk that impacted her from Elder Faust praising the many sacrifices women make for their husbands and children. Elder Scott acknowledged that women often take a husband's name and move away from family and friends to support a spouse's career. Still more, they endure the often tedious work of raising children, and to a degree that men usually do not. While praising women's many sacrifices, Elder Scott concluded: "You do all of these things willingly, *because you are a woman*."[1]

Audrey took comfort in this talk. It felt like a recognition of the hard, often unseen work of being a stay-at-home mother. But she also understood that talks like these weren't merely acknowledgments of women's contributions—they were also declarations about who women should be. In other words, she internalized the idea that to be true to their "divine nature," women will willingly set aside their desires in the service of others.

Lacking confidence in her own judgment, Audrey placed her hope in obedience—trusting it would guarantee everything would work out in the end. But now, beneath the betrayal of her husband was a deeper reckoning—she was confronting the ways she had betrayed herself, her own intuition and judgment, through her full surrender to others to guide her life.

Similar to the messages Audrey received, I remember Young Women lessons celebrating girls who gave up what they wanted to support the efforts of their priesthood-bearing brothers. We listened to stories of women sacrificing career aspirations for the sake of marriage and childrearing—decisions that were held up as expressions of faith and devotion. And these messages were strongly reinforced by prophetic counsel to women at the time to leave the workplace and return to the more noble calling of homemaker.

Several of the men I dated while attending Brigham Young University reminded me that pursuing graduate school should not take priority over finding a suitable marriage partner and starting a family. An LDS-themed pop song at the time put a fine point on it: "Mom you gave up your Ph.D., just because you loved me . . . ." All of these messages deeply shaped how many Latter-day Saints—including myself—understood what it meant to be a righteous woman in the church. There was only one legitimate way to fulfill that role, and it left little room for alternatives paths.

Again, motherhood is an exceptionally important vocation. Women often make considerable sacrifices for their children, setting aside both short-term pleasures and long-term aspirations to ensure their children's well-being. What's more, we all depend upon and benefit from this kind of care, even as these sacrifices are too often overlooked and undervalued by society. The support and recognition by our church leaders of women's significant contributions to families and society is welcomed and very important.

However, when self-denial is framed as *the* measure of feminine virtue—the defining trait of an ideal woman—we compromise women's ability to know themselves and choose their own paths. Equating virtue with self-denial fosters women's unnecessary dependence on others—especially men—to define a woman's identity and worth. And when religious instruction emphasizes motherhood and wifehood as forms of obedience, we limit women's ability to know their hearts and minds and unique potential beyond those roles. This narrow framing not only limits how women see themselves but also encourages economic and psychological dependence, ultimately undermining their agency and strength. As Russell M. Nelson said, "we need [women's] strength!" and we need women to "rise to [their] full stature, to fulfill the measure of [their] creation."[2] Women cannot do this if we encourage their relational deference and dependency in the name of humility and virtue.

Again, the explicitness of these gendered messages has softened significantly in recent years. We see more references to the importance of women's voices and women's contributions outside of the home. Yet, much of the adult membership of the church continues to operate and understand

56

themselves within these traditionally defined roles. Adult Latter-day Saint women fill my workshops looking to understand and undo an orientation to life that has yielded self-doubt and limited their ability to create an intimate marriage and joyful life.

We can absolutely value motherhood while still affirming individuality and the importance of personal choice in the pursuit of a moral life. If we want women to truly enjoy an inner strength and spiritual depth, we must place less value on compliance and more value on agency and individual integrity. We can value sacrifice for the sake of others without teaching women to self-deny. We can teach the value of learning from wise others without encouraging women to reflexively defer to men or external authority figures. When deference becomes the default, it undermines women's ability to know their own hearts and minds and make choices they can stand by.

As we'll discuss in a later chapter, we all begin life looking to adults and peers to know what to believe and how to act. Borrowing wisdom from and pleasing others is intuitive for most of us and largely benefits our early development. However, it is a significant mistake to identify this early inclination as the pinnacle of virtue. Obedience is the *first* law of heaven—as in an initial law—the starting place of a moral self in the world. Cultural messaging that encourages women to surrender their own judgment in the name of faith, or their desires in the name of selflessness, hinders the

57

self-trust we all need to be at peace with ourselves and integrate our desires.

What follows are examples of the specific meanings around ideal womanhood and sex that research participants and clients internalized, which interfered with these important spiritual and relational aims.

IT IS BETTER TO GIVE THAN RECEIVE

As depicted in Rachel's story, many LDS women believe that being *needless and wantless* are signature feminine virtues. I regularly ask women at my workshops if they are more comfortable giving or receiving. A strikingly large percentage say they much prefer to give. They tell me that "serving others" makes them feel valuable—*necessary*—while receiving makes them anxious. They are not sure they are worthy of care, and importantly, they don't want to be seen (or see themselves) as "needy" or "weak." Many women prefer the perceived control of being the giver over the anticipated vulnerability of receiving. (This is especially true in sex.)

Not only does receiving run counter to many women's internalized sense of who they ought to be, so too does the act of pursuing one's desires. As Caroline, a participant in one of my workshops, wrote: "Thinking about what I desire brings me to tears. I have guilt associated with wanting—wanting versus doing what is right or dutiful." Like many women I work with, Caroline viewed personal desire as fundamentally at odds with

58

righteousness. In her mind, "wanting" stood in opposition to "doing what is right." *Desire*, for her, was inherently selfish, while deferring to God's will—or prioritizing another's needs—was framed as selfless, and therefore virtuous.

Not only does our idealization of self-sacrifice make it exceptionally difficult for LDS women to reconcile their desires with spirituality, it also interferes with the development of self-referencing and self-trust. "I don't trust desire," another workshop participant wrote. "I don't trust that my desires are the *right* ones. . . . I am afraid to make choices!" If we are afraid of our desires—afraid to understand or consider them—we cannot benefit from the information contained within them. And we need that information to understand ourselves and make life decisions we can stand by. Without this crucial self-awareness—without access to this important internal compass—we will remain dependent upon others to tell us who to be and what is right.

NEVER SAY NO

Consistent with the idealization of the selfless, deferential female, many LDS women have learned that sexual desire is not feminine or virtuous. Instead, they have been taught to attend to their husband's "sexual needs." In fact, in my dissertation research exploring LDS women's relationship to their sexuality, most women spoke about sex in terms of their husband's desires and rarely as something

59

meaningful to them personally. Much like Rachel's pre-wedding sex education, several women told me of advice from a parent along the same lines: "Never say 'no' to your husband." It's not an exaggeration to say that heeding this advice will make passionate, desire-based sex impossible.

Having sex because you understand it as your obligation leads invariably to the deadening of authentic desire. Sexual desire thrives on freedom and choice. When women learn to self-deny—when they orient to life from a frame of duty—they are thwarted in their ability to value and integrate their sexuality. This hinders women's ability to embrace their desires and pleasures and let themselves be cared for sexually by a spouse. It also impedes their ability to grow into a whole person—to be at peace with themselves—and to experience a spirituality that allows for self-acceptance and soulful pleasure.

THE IMPORTANCE OF BEING DESIRABLE

Although we tend to sidestep the reality of women's sexual desire in our faith culture, we do focus on women's desirability. Women in my research had absorbed the idea that men are naturally driven by sexual *desire*, and women should make themselves *desirable* (to men). To be desirable, women learned they should be physically attractive and embody the above-mentioned ideals of selflessness and kindness. But beyond these qualities, most women I interviewed also understood desirability through the lens of sexual purity. Chastity, they told me, wasn't just a standard to live by; it was a measure of their value. Their sense of self-worth and their expectations of how others—especially men—would perceive them was deeply shaped by their ability to meet this ideal.

The fact that women linked chastity with their value is not surprising given how much our instruction to young women has emphasized it. Women spoke of object lessons such as chewed gum and crushed flowers that represented the tarnishing of their desirability through sexual experience. Elizabeth Smart, who was kidnapped and raped at the age of fourteen, had also been taught these kinds of object lessons. They made such a strong impression that she believed there was little point in trying to escape her captor because she now saw herself as worthless—no more valuable than "a chewed-up piece of gum."[3] Women in my research described viewing themselves as "damaged goods" for having any sexual experience—even when it was coerced or unchosen.

Although such lessons are intended to underscore the value of chastity, they cause great damage by teaching that a woman's inherent worth is tied to her sexual experience—when in fact, it is not. And the idea that there is no true repentance ("You can repaint a fence but you can't hide the holes") runs counter to the core message of the gospel. Lessons such as these must be abandoned if we are to be truer to women and truer to the principles of our faith.[4]

In response to these teachings, several women in my research chose to conceal their sexual histories from their husbands, despite having repented and believing they had been forgiven by God. They didn't imagine a spouse would be so gracious. Many had been taught that their sexuality was something to be preserved for a future spouse—so why would he accept it having been shared elsewhere? Notably, they often did not hold their husbands to the same standard they applied to themselves. They said it would be more understandable if a husband had engaged in premarital sexual behavior. Of course, this double standard is not theological; we believe in repentance and profess a single standard of sexual behavior for men and women. But we often promote a *cultural* double standard—one that many women (and men) have perceived and lived by.

Our focus on women's desirability and devaluation of their desires means women simply have a difficult time thinking of themselves as legitimate sexual beings. Several clients have said to me some version of the following: "I cannot imagine a woman who is both 'spiritual' *and* sexual—I mean a righteous woman who *really* enjoys sex. The two just do not go together in my mind." Naturally, tying a woman's value to sexual innocence hinders her ability to accept and develop her sexual self, making it difficult to even envision a reality where spirituality and sexuality can coexist. If we continue to use fear and shame as a teacher, we may get a young woman to the altar as a virgin, but fully interfere with her ability to be at peace within herself and relate to sex as a soulful, intimate act.

IS MODEST *TRULY* HOTTEST?

Another significant barrier to women's sexual integration lies in how we teach modesty. At its core, true modesty reflects a lived awareness of the inherent worth of every soul. A modest person lives in the truth that despite our varying skills and resources, we are all alike unto God. Whether we enjoy wealth, intelligence, beauty, or any other advantage, to be modest is to remain humble about that relative strength. Truly modest individuals don't flaunt their gifts or use them to take advantage of others; instead, they treat everyone with dignity and respect.

In our collective unease about sex, however, we have made the principle of modesty almost entirely about sexual modesty—and specifically, *female* sexual modesty—obsessing over how women dress and present themselves. In church lessons, we often tell women to cover their bodies because it is important to help *men* resist temptation.☞ This misinterpretation of modesty's moral value

---

☞ As an example, in a lesson entitled "Teaching Chastity and Modesty," women are taught that "anything that causes improper thoughts . . . is not modest. It is especially important that we teach young girls not to wear clothes that would encourage young men to have improper thoughts. Modesty can help us keep our chastity." (The Latter-Day Saint Woman: Basic Manual, 2000).

not only distorts its true meaning, but also blurs the lines of personal responsibility in interactions between men and women.

Teaching women to cover their bodies for the sake of men sends several troubling messages. First, it implies that sexual attraction is inherently a problem rather than a natural and meaningful part of life. Second, it places the burden of men's thoughts and behaviors on women, holding them responsible for something ultimately beyond their control. While women *are* responsible for their own motivations and choices, it is misguided to tell women that their attractiveness makes men feel things they shouldn't feel, and therefore women must prevent those feelings from occurring.

Placing the burden on women to manage men's responses not only diverts men from the essential developmental work of recognizing and wisely navigating their own sexual feelings—a crucial step toward sexual integrity—but it also conveys a harmful message to women: that men are not able to handle their sexual urges.

Inevitably, this belief erodes trust in men—and in one's spouse—undermining the foundation of a collaborative, mutually fulfilling sexual relationship. If women believe they must monitor their partner's choices, it interferes with the psychological freedom that is so critical to desirable sex. A married client, Stephanie, put it this way: "I want to 'let go' in sex, but I feel like I can't. Jake has struggled with porn in the past, and I'm afraid if I fully surrender to my own feelings, he'll take that as permission to surrender to all of his. And, well, who would keep things from going off the rails, in that case?"

The truth is that women can value their sexuality and their desirability and be modest about both. Modesty should not be about shame or fear of the body; it is instead an expression of self-respect and respect for others. It's not defined by the existence of a sleeve or the length of a skirt but by an inner disposition: a sense of peace with oneself. When we are at peace with who we are, we can appreciate our bodies and beauty without needing to flaunt or extract validation from others. In the best understanding of the principle, sexual modesty allows us to value our sexuality by being discriminating about who we share our bodies and sexuality with.

Our theology teaches us that *both* men and women are expected to be chaste and to choose wisely with this remarkable gift. While there are cultural forces that encourage a sexual double standard, we believe in a *single* standard of sexual behavior. And while we too often use shame and fear to the detriment of our sexual development, we can offer principles of modesty, chastity, and sexual self-control in ways that facilitate our self-acceptance, wise decision-making, and sexual integration.

LDS WOMEN WHO THRIVE

In my dissertation research I looked at the question of LDS women's sexual agency. Given some of the troubling cultural messages about the incompatibility of femininity and sexuality, I wanted to see how married women who had grown up in the church were faring in their sexual relationships. Were they at peace with their sexuality? Were they able to create a sexual relationship that they desired and enjoyed?

Most of the women I interviewed struggled under the cultural double standard I have outlined above. They had internalized messages that framed femininity and sexual desire as incompatible, implicitly validating desire more in men than in women. Many assumed greater responsibility than their male partners for sexual missteps—even in situations involving coercion. As a result, they struggled to acknowledge and honor their own desires, both inside and outside of marriage.

Although most women struggled to integrate their sexuality and be agents of it, there was a subset of LDS women who had *not* internalized this cultural double standard. They were at peace with sex and enjoyed it. They did not see a contradiction between their sexual pleasure and their spirituality. Although I didn't use this language at the time of my research, looking back, these women had achieved a meaningful level of sexual integration. They were agents of their sexuality—neither controlled by it nor afraid of it.

What can we learn from these LDS women? They understood several important things about themselves and their sexuality: They viewed sex as a

66

gift—not as a gift to a husband *through* them, but a gift from God to them, and recognized the value of their own pleasure. They also saw themselves as fundamentally equal to men. Even when they regarded their husbands as the "leader of the home," they still functioned as true partners—equal in both decision-making and responsibility. In other words, they took their desires and beliefs seriously (as did the men they were married to).

They also believed the law of chastity worked in their favor because it facilitated the kind of sexual relationship they desired—one rooted in commitment and care. The expectation of sex in marriage allowed them to enjoy sex with partners who weren't just interested in sex, but interested in *them*—interested in their happiness and in their whole being.

In my interviews, I asked women about their first awareness of sexual arousal—feelings usually discovered on their own when they were young. Most of the women I interviewed regarded their first arousal as a negative thing—something inherently "dirty" or "bad." However, the women who had integrated their sexuality, the women who thrived, related to their first arousal as positive—something they were excited about. Even though they were unmarried at the time, they looked forward to developing and expressing these feelings more once married.

Rather than viewing the law of chastity as something that diminished sex, or as something to obey to earn men's approval, these women saw it as a principle that safeguarded their wellbeing. They were not compelled by the promises of the sexual revolution—particularly the separation of sex from commitment or love. Instead, they believed that linking sex with commitment was more likely to lead to the kind of life they desired. In their view, expecting men to channel their sexuality in service of women and family—rather than for self-gratification—was a standard that ultimately worked in their favor.

They chose to follow the law of chastity out of their own desire and personal agency—in a self-defining way. They did not confuse conservative sexual behavior with sexual shame, nor did they confuse it with sexism. They expected the same chaste behavior of men as they did of themselves. They did not coddle or accommodate men at the expense of themselves or their larger desires, whether dating or married.

These same women were more likely to succeed in living the law of chastity because it aligned with their authentic desires—not because they were seeking the approval of a future spouse. Their commitment stemmed from a place of self-respect and personal conviction. By taking their own desires seriously, they were better prepared to cultivate a sexual relationship rooted in mutual respect. They carried a clear sense of their own worth and chose partners who recognized and valued them similarly.

Together, these couples were able to build collaborative and fulfilling sexual relationships—ones that reflected the dignity and desires of both partners. While I did not study the question of *why* some women were able to integrate their sexuality and others were not, it was clear that their self-determining approach—based in a strong sense of personal worth—was central to their happiness. Valuing themselves and their desires laid the groundwork for their sexual integration and marital happiness.

We can hold up sexuality and pleasure as important parts of being female and, when anchored in love and commitment, part of our happiness and spiritual sustenance. We can relate to our faith and our sexuality in ways that bless our lives and increase our joy. However, the messages directed at women are not the only challenge we face. LDS men, too, have received limiting and misleading messages that have undermined their sexual integration and their ability to foster genuine intimacy in marriage. We'll turn to them next.

CHAPTER 2: SELF-REFLECTION QUESTIONS

1. Consider the cultural messages about femininity and sexuality explored in this chapter. Which messages did you internalize?

2. How did these received ideas shape your perceptions of yourself as a woman? How did they shape your perspectives on sex? How did they shape your choices?

3. How have you related to sexual desire over the course of your life? Are you comfortable viewing yourself as a sexual being? In what ways has your relationship to sex and desire shaped your connection with yourself and with your spouse?

4. Consider the women in the research with higher sexual integration. Are there ways that these women related to themselves and sex that would be more empowering or beneficial for you to emulate?

\- -

\- -

\- -

\- -

\- -

\- -

\- -

SHAME & SUPPRESSION: THE SILENT STRUGGLE OF MEN

3

"We were taught not to lick the cupcake or crush the flower."

When teaching the Marriage and Family Relations class in church one Sunday, I spoke about some of the object lessons on chastity that women in my dissertation research had received as young women—lessons designed to demonstrate that sexual behavior lessens a woman's desirability to a man. These lessons made sexually experienced women equivalent in desirability to half-eaten cupcakes and mangled flowers. Because I'd never been in a young men's classroom, I asked the adult men if they had ever received any such messages—messages instructing them that sexual behavior would undermine their desirability to a future wife. They all said no, and then one man exclaimed comically, "We were taught not to *lick* the cupcake or *crush* the flower!" His humorous statement captured the implicit meaning many of us have internalized: Men are the sexual actors—the lickers and the crushers—and women are acted upon. It also communicates that men's sexuality corrupts women.

Unlike women, men are taught to see themselves as sexual beings and sexual agents. In contrast to women, they are offered an identity that includes sexual desire. Men can be both masculine *and*

sexual. While this may be better than the delegit-
imizing messages given to women explored in
chapter 2—that femininity and sexual desire don't
mix—the messages offered to men can also interfere with self-acceptance and sexual integration.

Men are indeed taught through our gender-role
instruction that they have the power to act—that
they naturally lead and *affect*. But as the actors or
pursuers in the sexual realm, men also learn they
have the power to destroy what is innocent and virtuous. So, sexual desire may be part of being a man,
but it's also his potential downfall and may keep
him from fulfilling his priesthood responsibilities.
Like many women, LDS men often harbor deep
ambivalence about their sexual nature and struggle
to see how it could be a part of a moral life—how it
might be connected to love.

Of course, men can indeed do harm with their
sexuality. And hedonistic pleasure for its own
sake, without any moral framing or higher aim,
will undermine a relationship and a person's spiritual peace. Men (and women) must learn how
to choose wisely with their sexuality to become
capable of sexual love and intimacy. Yet, in all our
cultural anxiety about human eroticism, we are
quick to equate sexual arousal with sin—instill-
ing in young men a deep and unnecessary anxiety
about their sexuality.

Conflating sexual feeling with sin interferes
with our larger goal of self-acceptance and sexual
self-control. In truth, men can learn to love deeply

74

through their sexuality. They can offer a generous acceptance and celebration of the feminine in ways that deeply enrich a couple's emotional and spiritual bond. But our collective panic around eroticism interferes with this larger goal. When boys are taught to fear their sexual nature, it can lead to increased preoccupation with sex and non-intimate sexual behavior. In our anxious attempts to prevent sin, we can unintentionally undermine young men's ability to integrate their sexuality and make loving, conscious choices with it—capacities that are essential to building an intimate and wholehearted marriage.

THE PROBLEM OF "IMPURE THOUGHTS"

Too many young boys incorrectly learn that normal sexual interest, emerging in force in early adolescence, corrupts the soul. Men in my courses talk about growing up believing that sexual thoughts were an implicit form of sin. In the 1990 *For the Strength of Youth* pamphlet (the pamphlet that many adult Latter-day saints grew up with), we learned ". . .[S]exual sins are more serious than any other sins except murder or denying the Holy Ghost." We also learned we should "pray to the Lord, who will help [us] resist temptation and overcome inappropriate thoughts and feelings."

Many young men interpreted statements like these to mean that sexual feelings in and of themselves made them unclean and unworthy. As one male course participant wrote: "I remember feeling that I was the most vile human on earth because I had those exact thoughts and desires that the leaders were talking about. I was sure I was the dregs of evil." Another course member wrote, "I remember feeling so broken because I couldn't control my thoughts as a youth. I thought God was so disappointed with me that I prayed He would delete my sexual desires. And while I never seriously thought about self-harm, the connection between lust and plucking your eye out did cause the thought to cross my mind." In my work with adult men, this unfortunate interpretation of our messaging is very common.

To be sure, some church leaders and teachers have clearly affirmed that sexual feelings are not inherently wrong, emphasizing that it's our choices—not the feelings themselves—that truly matter. Yet many LDS men never heard or fully absorbed those messages of acceptance. Instead, they were inundated with fear-based teachings that portrayed sex and pleasure as fundamentally corrosive to the soul.

Several adult men shared that hearing messages normalizing and accepting sexual feelings would have made a meaningful difference in their development. As one man put it, "It would have been reassuring to hear someone say, 'You're alright. You're normal. That happens to all of us. Here's what you can do. . . .' Instead, I hid my sexual thoughts and feelings and rejected myself. I was left to create my own meanings, many of which were unhealthy and unhelpful. Over time I developed so much self-loathing. Looking back, it's clear how much support and reassurance could have made a difference."

It is harmful to teach young people that their emerging, unchosen sexuality is at odds with God or goodness. Suggesting that our divine sexual nature threatens our basic worthiness is particularly unjust when we know it would indeed be unusual for a thirteen-year-old *not* to have sexual thoughts.

And while we must make distinctions between feelings and behavior as an important starting place, it is also true that behaviors like self-stimulation are normal for adolescents. Young people are imperfectly navigating their emerging arousal and emotions. Yet when young men masturbate, as many do, it is usually treated as a serious moral failing, one that can limit their participation in priesthood responsibilities. Because these priesthood activities are typically public, being excluded opens the door to social scrutiny and judgment. And already insecure boys can feel shame and self-rejection over behavior that is, in reality, fairly typical.

My client Jared struggled with masturbation in his adolescence. Despite his sincere efforts to stop, he found himself unable to fully overcome it. He knew that confessing his struggle to his bishop would likely result in losing the privilege of passing the sacrament—a consequence that would draw the attention of his parents and peers. The prospect of such public exposure felt unbearable, so Jared usually chose to hide the truth instead. This left him with a heavy burden of guilt—not just for the behavior itself, but also for deceiving someone he admired. Quietly, Jared began to internalize the belief that he was fundamentally flawed, and that his sexuality was at the core of his brokenness.

It is true that making wise choices in response to sexual feelings is essential for healthy relationships and lasting peace of mind. Developing the ability to manage our sexual impulses is critical to building marriages grounded in trust and authentic desire. However, we undermine this important developmental task when we rely on fear and social shame as primary tools for guiding behavior.

The idea that *any* arousal or pleasure interferes with a moral life creates unnecessary anxiety that interferes with our broader relational and spiritual aims. In fact, avoiding sexual feelings out of fear can disrupt our psychosexual development, hindering the growth required for both psychological and spiritual maturity. If a person cannot learn to accept and regulate himself in the presence of sexual feelings, he will struggle to cultivate genuine inner peace. And if he cannot see sexuality as a positive part of being a man, he won't be able to share it and love a spouse through it.

PERFECT OBEDIENCE BRINGS SEXUAL ANXIETY

In his desire to live the law of chastity "perfectly," my thirty-two-year-old client, Samuel, did *nothing* that would arouse sexual feelings in his body. Taking this directive from the *For the Strength of Youth* pamphlet, he committed in his early adolescence to obey the standards set out in the guide flawlessly. He did all he could to stay away from sexual feelings whatsoever. This meant he avoided touching his own genitals entirely, afraid that even incidental contact might create feelings he shouldn't have. As he grew older, Samuel's caution extended to his social relationships. He chose not to date to avoid the inevitable feelings of attraction that women stirred in him. Instead, he filled his time with video games where he felt more in control of his emotions.

Samuel was intelligent and even well-employed—realities that might suggest a trajectory of independence. But he was still living with his parents in his early thirties when he reached out for help. His rigorous avoidance of arousal had stunted his psychological and relational growth. Rather than being a source of strength, his perfect obedience to the law of chastity had kept him from forging the emotional maturity and self-confidence he needed to leave his father and mother and cleave unto another.

Recognizing Samuel's scrupulosity, I suggested in our first meeting that no church leader intended for him to take such a strict interpretation of the pamphlet. Clearly, there is room to be human, I said. But Samuel pointed out that my interpretation was not what was actually written: "Do not do *anything* to arouse the powerful emotions that must be expressed only in marriage," he quoted. "Do not participate in talk or activities that arouse sexual feelings." He also reminded me that church leaders emphasize perfect obedience as the key to receiving blessings. And Samuel wanted the blessings.

Perfect Obedience Brings Sexual Anxiety Samuel was suffering with OCD-type tendencies focused on his fear of sexuality. His approach was therefore more literal and scrupulous than most church members and more extreme than any reasonable church leader would intend. But the form of his interpretation serves as a case in point: His story not only lays bare our conflation of sexual feeling and sin, it also shows that Samuel's pursuit of perfect obedience—doing *nothing* that would create arousal—was working against him. In truth, "failing" to live this obediently would have been a blessing for Samuel.

Samuel's avoidance was limiting his growth into adulthood—undermining his self-acceptance and his capacity for genuine intimacy. In contrast, those who acknowledge their sexual feelings and make thoughtful choices in response to them are better able to integrate this aspect of themselves and find peace with it. Speaking as if sexual feelings are a problem or as if full suppression is the goal can cause complicated and long-term damage.

Upon returning from his mission, another client, James, reported to his bishop that he had never in his life masturbated. James was telling the truth, but his bishop didn't believe him. The bishop's incredulity exposes the implicit expectation many of us have that our youth will *not* succeed in abiding by our expectations around sexual self-restraint. What, then, is the purpose of stating them in such exacting terms? When we present perfect obedience—essentially complete sexual repression—as the ideal, despite knowing it's neither fully attainable nor leads to an end we desire, we needlessly increase the self-rejection of young, insecure boys—individuals already in an uneasy relationship with their transforming bodies and identities. This sets up our youth to fail and falsely believe they are disappointing God for being the sexual creatures they were designed to be.

While many of us have taught these restrictive ideas about sex to our children, most of us intuitively understand that part of growing into adulthood involves experiencing and exploring sexual feelings. Although this fact scares many of us, it's a necessary part of understanding one's sexuality—and fundamental to romance and partnering. We don't serve our kids well when we vilify sexual curiosity. It is neither honest nor helpful to the goal of sexual integration. Offering an ideal that is neither truly ideal nor realistically attainable except by compromising oneself is damaging to our spiritual wellbeing. It also encourages hiding and suppression in the name of righteousness. As one course participant wrote, "If I had been reassured that my experiences were normal, I would have learned honesty from parents and leaders. Instead, I learned the implicit idea that suppression, hiding, and lying about my thoughts and feelings were the only path to perfection."

SEXUAL REPRESSION DRIVES OUR OBSESSION

Not only does fear-based repression interfere with self-acceptance, it can actually *increase* our preoccupation with sex. This, of course, is the opposite of what we hope to achieve. Excessive fear inhibits the self-awareness we need to temper and integrate our impulses. Trying *not* to think about something forbidden means you must think about it.

Thirteen-year-old Joey learned in church that masturbation was a sin. Eager to do what is right, he tried earnestly to push down these newly emerging feelings. But his inability to suppress them led him to obsess over the sexual desires he shouldn't have (and couldn't obliterate). Soon enough, normal sexual interest turned into obsessive preoccupation. The harder Joey tried to silence his desires, the more relentless they became—and the more often he found himself giving into them.

More consequential than the masturbation itself was the fact that Joey's self-hatred was deepening. His overwhelming sense of shame made it difficult for him to be self-aware, even though self-awareness is what he most needed to guide his decisions. Instead, Joey simply grew to loathe his sexuality and himself. Once a carefree pre-adolescent boy, he now believed he would never be as good as the other (less honest) deacons who, unlike him, passed the sacrament each Sunday. In his isolation and self-re-jection, masturbation was both a tempting reprieve from the anxiety that dominated his life now and an ongoing source of torment. The belief that his sexual desires were implicitly sinful led to years of suffering in a disrupted relationship with himself, his sexuality, and God.

Unfortunately, Joey's experience is far from uncommon. When we treat normal feelings and desires as abnormal, we foster a self-rejection that can intensify sexual fixation. If we want to reduce sexual preoccupation and increase our ability to manage sexual impulses wisely, it's essential that we talk about masturbation and the draw to sexu-ally explicit material as *normal* desires rather than *deviant* ones, even as we encourage better choices. Our goal isn't to eliminate desire, but to foster self-awareness and self-acceptance—foundations for making thoughtful, values-based decisions.

In addition to driving our sexual preoccupation, shaming sexual desire can also make non-intimate eroticism more compelling than it would otherwise be. When a man views his sexuality as a shameful part of himself, or as an unwelcome burden on a woman, he may be more inclined to emotionally disconnected forms of sex. A woman on screen, for example, never says no, always desires sex, and makes his sexuality okay. Although the dynamic is clearly artificial, its appeal becomes more under-standable when viewed against the backdrop of messages many men receive—messages that frame their sexuality as dangerous, unwelcome, or inherently harmful.

When a man lacks a clear vision of what a reciprocal, intimate relationship can be—how it can enrich a woman's life and how he plays a role in making that possible—he may drift toward more hedonistic expressions of sex, ultimately undermining his own peace of mind.

MEN'S INTIMATE AMBIVALENCE

As we've explored, many men carry a sense of shame around their sexuality, often viewing it as a lesser or even problematic part of themselves. So while they may appear to be the more eager partners in a sexual relationship, their outward enthusiasm can mask a deep ambivalence—not just about their sexuality, but about their own worthiness. Compared to a more sexually hesitant spouse, these men might seem confident, even dominant, but true peace with their sexuality—and with themselves—is often still elusive.

Bradley was deeply frustrated. He complained often that his wife, Andrea, was rarely in the mood for sex. Despite knowing it made her uncomfortable, he pushed for new sexual positions and experiences, framing her resistance as a refusal to meet his needs or show him that he mattered. From Andrea's point of view, Bradley was demanding and insatiable, more intent on taking from her than genuinely connecting.

Though she often consented, it wasn't out of desire—it was to manage his anger and despair. Beneath Bradley's entitlement and judgment was an insecure man desperate for affirmation. And his neediness and pressure turned sex into a chore for Andrea—something to be endured rather than enjoyed. Rather than bringing them closer, their physical intimacy was steadily driving an ever-deeper wedge between them.

When they met with me, Bradley focused on his wife's limited interest in sex as the major challenge in their relationship. "I bought her your course on desire for women, and she hasn't even started it yet," he complained. From his perspective, Andrea's low desire seemed to be the root of their sexual struggles. But underneath Bradley's focus on his wife's shortcomings lay deep, unspoken insecurities of his own. He struggled with self-loathing and carried significant anxiety about sex. Rather than confronting those feelings directly, he placed the burden on Andrea—believing, and often insisting, that if she desired him the way she was "supposed" to, he would feel okay.

During a couples' session, Bradley mentioned in passing that he felt rejected by God. It seemed almost tangential, but I sensed this belief was important. I suggested that Bradley write out a dialogue with God—an imagined conversation about his sexuality. When Bradley presented me with this written interaction, it was evident how much the God in his mind was rejecting and disgusted with his sexual desires. The exercise proved eye-opening for Bradley as well. He realized he envisioned a God that had no tolerance for his pleasure or happiness—one who, in many ways, mirrored his own father: stern, exacting, and unyielding.

Bradley reflected in our conversations on the admiration he had for his dad when he was a young boy. He wanted his dad's acceptance and attention more than anything and yet never seemed able to get it. He looked forward to his father's return each day, but his efforts to engage him were usually met with rejection and distance if not explicit disdain.

Through our conversations, Bradley began to recognize the depth of his own self-rejection, his core belief that he was unlovable—if his own father couldn't accept him, he reasoned, why would anyone else?—and that he was handling this fear through sexual entitlement. In other words, pressuring Andrea to accommodate him sexually was an intuitive, albeit destructive, solution. Much like his father, Bradley used demand and subtle contempt to shield himself from the implications of his wife's agency. At times, he had even initiated sexual encounters that he knew Andrea didn't truly desire or derive pleasure from, insisting at the time that this made him feel "closer" to her. When challenged later, he conceded that it was the illusion of control that gave him temporary relief—the fantasy that he could extract her acceptance.

Ultimately, Bradley's sense of entitlement was creating emotional distance between them—leaving his wife feeling uneasy, disconnected, and less inclined to engage with him. Ironically, his efforts to protect himself from rejection were pushing Andrea further away, only deepening the very fear he was trying to avoid.

"SEXUAL NEEDS" SUFFOCATE DESIRE

Most men want to feel desired and welcomed by their wives, which is why intimate rejection can feel so painfully personal. This is especially true when there's no alternative source of affirmation and no way to compel desire. Being desired is deeply affirming, but it also exposes our lack of control; we can't make someone want us, no matter how much we might wish otherwise.

Much like Bradley, many men cope with this vulnerability through a culturally supported entitlement in marriage. That is, they use the idea of "sexual needs" to pressure their wives to accommodate them. This mindset is understandable given the cultural messages that designate women as natural need-fulfillers. However, this approach is a recipe for failure. When sex is treated as a duty, it cannot be about desire. A spouse may comply, but she won't genuinely desire—and for most men, it's distressing to be with someone who feels obligated rather than eager to be close.

Of course, when sex is about managing needs, it can't create the sense of passion or intimate friendship that couples are seeking in their marriages.

And it is ultimately humiliating to feel that sex is offered out of obligation. So, while some men push for sexual accommodation to avoid the despair of rejection, they create a reality in which rejection is nearly inevitable. As one course participant wrote, "I believed it was my wife's job to take care of my sexuality. I spent almost twenty years pressuring her to do that for me and resenting her for not being able or willing. I blamed her for 'forcing me' to suppress my desires and feel like a hedonistic monster. I wasted so many years and damaged my most important relationship because of this belief."

FEAR IS A POOR MOTIVATOR

Physician and researcher Dean Ornish says, in reference to dietary behavior change, that the fear of dying is not as compelling a motivation as is the joy of living. I imagine a similar principle is true for the pleasures of sex. Fear of hell is not as motivating as the joy of intimate friendship. To facilitate our sexual self-regulation and integration, we would do better (for ourselves and our children) to focus on the desirable outcomes of choosing wisely with our sexuality.

We must believe and teach that sexuality—while unwieldy and sometimes overwhelming—is a genuine gift. It is a capacity that awakens us and connects us to the sensual richness of the world. Our relational and spiritual growth requires us to integrate and channel this gift so that it can be a source of peace and soulful pleasure in our lives.

Like mastering any new skill, the process can feel awkward and humbling at first. Consider learning to ski: at the beginning, the skis seem to control us more than we control them, and staying upright can feel impossible. Inevitably, we stumble—falling at the exit from the lift or venturing onto trails beyond our ability. Yet, through our missteps, we eventually gain the skill and confidence to navigate with grace. Over time, we harness the power of the skis and, in doing so, discover a whole new realm of joy and pleasure.

Even experienced skiers remain mindful of the risks that come with navigating the slopes of a mountain, but their mastery and earned confidence allows them to more fully enjoy the experience. Similarly, to find joy in our sexuality, we must approach it as a process of integration—learning from our missteps, forgiving ourselves, and focusing on the ultimate goal: the creation of loving, committed, and life-giving sexual intimacy.

The good news is that official church instruction around sexuality is improving. The recently revised *For the Strength of Youth* pamphlet—now with the subtitle: *A Guide for Making Choices*—explicitly articulates the value of sexual desire: "Sexual feelings are an important part of God's plan. These feelings are not sinful—they are sacred." It also focuses on the importance of choices, explaining that the purpose of the guide is "not to give you a 'yes' or 'no' about every possible choice you might face," but instead to help you make wise decisions while being thoughtful and prayerful.

Fear is a Poor Motivator Additionally, the guide has moved away from using fear as a motivator for sexual restraint—a feature of the 2011 *For the Strength of Youth* pamphlet, which warned that "sexual sins are more serious than any other sins except murder or denying the Holy Ghost." The new guide emphasizes the benefits of the law of chastity, such as how it "will bring greater love, trust and unity to your marriage." These elements are essential to our acceptance of our sexuality and our ability to make choices in line with our highest values—which is to say, these elements support the goal of our sexual integration.

Before considering how we can create a richer integration of our sexuality and spirituality through our personal development and the integration of our sexual feelings, let's consider in the next chapter how the cultural false traditions articulated in chapters 2 and 3 conspire to undermine desire, intimacy and authentic joy in marriage. These are marital stories and experiences that are all too common to us.

CHAPTER 3: SELF-REFLECTION QUESTIONS

1. Reflecting on the cultural messages about men and sexuality explored in this chapter, which messages impacted you in particular?

2. How did these ideas shape your view of yourself as a man and sexual being? How did they shape your view of the opposite sex?

3. How have you related to sexual desire throughout your life? Are you comfortable seeing yourself as a sexual person? How has this orientation to sex and desire impacted your relationship to yourself and to a spouse?

4. Were there leaders or parents who gave you positive ideas about sexuality that have been helpful to you? If so, what were those ideas?

ROLE-PLAYING IN MARRIAGE

4

*"Seeing myself through the unblinking eyes
of an intimate, intelligent other, an honest
spouse, is humiliating beyond anticipation."*
—Michael Novak

Emmy reached out hoping to meet with me as soon as possible. Just days earlier, in a raw and difficult conversation, her husband Marc confessed to viewing pornography throughout their thirteen-year marriage. The revelation landed like a punishing blow, upending everything she thought she knew about her husband and their marriage.

Marc was currently serving as the elders quorum president, which made his confession all the more disorienting. Emmy had believed she had married a man of unwavering faith—someone who lived above the coarser aspects of human nature. So, learning that Marc had been secretly viewing other women revealed a side of her husband that she had neither expected nor allowed herself to imagine. What had once seemed secure now appeared riddled with fractures, leaving her to wrestle with an unsettling question: Who was Marc, and what had their marriage really been about?

Given how devastating a pornography disclosure can be, we often treat pornography itself as the core marital problem. We tend to imagine the graphic content has taken hold of and corrupted the soul of its viewer. Certainly, a habit of non-intimate sexual indulgence will erode a person's inner peace and limit their tolerance of intimacy in marriage. But as this chapter will explore, pornography is more often a symptom of one's challenges with self-regulation and intimacy than it is the cause of them.

As human beings in an uncertain world, we naturally seek ways to escape the pressure and discomfort that come with honest engagement in our lives and relationships. Pornography, like many indulgent escapes, offers a fleeting hit of pleasure—a momentary reprieve from the pain of invalidation and the vulnerability of real connection. We are all tempted to protect our egos at the expense of exposure and growth. This can take the form of controlling others, avoiding vulnerability, or seeking gratification in ways that ultimately limit us. In fact, each of the temptations of Christ mirrors our own inclination to gratify the body and ego rather than submit to the refining work of the soul.

Though sparked by the pornography revelation, Marc and Emmy's crisis reveals deeper, ego-protective dynamics at work. As we examine their story, we'll explore how their relational patterns—often unconscious—led them to seek comfort and control in ways that ultimately stifled intimacy and hindered the growth of their marriage.

Emmy and Marc had always been conscientious members of the church. They each had served missions and placed great importance on marrying in the temple. Before their wedding, they were very careful about the amount of physical intimacy they allowed themselves, limiting their interactions to holding hands and brief kisses. Emmy knew she was more conscientious than many of her friends about these things, but her strong desire to do what is right drove her. She saw obedience as a means of securing God's guidance and protection in a world that often felt overwhelming to her.

Role-playing in Marriage

Not only had they been very cautious prior to marriage, they were careful within it, too. Just before the wedding, Emmy's mother told her that oral sex was not allowed for Latter-day Saints, pointing to a letter from the First Presidency issued in 1982. Emmy was curious about oral sex, so this news was disappointing. But wanting to do what is right, she unilaterally took the possibility off the table. Marc was unhappy about this, but he also didn't want to seem selfish or overly sexual, so he hid his disappointment and went along with her decision without complaint.

This was a typical pattern in their relationship: When Emmy felt anxious about something, she would often propose a standard and Marc would go along with it. One such rule involved R-rated movies. Emmy believed that avoiding them was essential to a spiritual atmosphere in their home. Because Marc wanted his wife's acceptance and hated making waves, he acquiesced despite lacking much personal conviction on the matter.

This accommodating disposition was intuitive for Marc. He had grown up in a family where his desires were seldom acknowledged. His parents were strict, and challenging them usually led to negative consequences. As a result, standing behind his own desires and beliefs while tolerating the disapproval of others seemed outside of his current capacity. He was very good at keeping the (superficial) peace—doing whatever made Emmy comfortable—while masking many of his contradictory thoughts and desires.

On one level, Marc very much liked accommodating Emmy. It was how he understood what a good husband does. It also gave him a sense of purpose and importance. And, as long as he was attending to *her* needs and fears, his insecurities were less obvious to both of them. It made him feel strong to be needed by her. The problem was that Emmy too easily placed the responsibility for her unhappiness on Marc. Having learned that a wife's role is to be dependent—and with little connection to her own agency—she readily looked to her husband to make things right.

Like many men, Marc didn't interpret his wife's unhappiness as a reflection of her own inner struggles. Instead, he saw it primarily as a judgment of him—evidence that he was falling short. This echoed his early experiences of not measuring up to his parents' high expectations, making Emmy's displeasure especially painful. But rather than reveal his distress, Marc pulled away, finding it easier to go silent than expose his feelings of inadequacy and fear.

With time, Marc found it increasingly difficult to desire and be sexually open to his (very attractive) wife. He tended to approach sex with the mindset that he needed to please Emmy, but this sense of obligation felt suffocating at times—like more of the same demand he felt in everyday life. If he ever approached Emmy in a way that was unexpected or not immediately to her liking, she would respond with critique, pressuring him to do whatever gave her comfort. Of course, Emmy had every right to say what she did and did not desire, but they struggled to collaborate—to work together as equals in creating a sexual relationship that felt meaningful to them both. With their shared belief that Emmy was more vulnerable, and therefore the one whose preferences needed to be accommodated, it was always sex on her terms.

Porn, on the other hand, provided an occasional escape for Marc—he experienced it as a place of relative freedom. As an adolescent in his high-demand family, he learned to hide the parts of himself that his parents would critique and control. In an environment where there was little room to sort out who he was, including his emerging sexual feelings, he learned a pattern of sexual behavior that was solitary and hidden. This less exposed way to be sexual continued to tempt Marc even in marriage. And he used his resentments to justify his secrecy, telling himself that he "gave so much" to keep Emmy happy that he deserved to take something for himself.

Even though Marc saw his tendency to be agreeable as a virtue, it didn't create any honest peace. In fact, continually deferring to Emmy's preferences left Marc feeling unappreciated and increasingly controlled. Over time, those feelings hardened into a quiet resentment—something Emmy could sense in his emotional distance but hesitated to confront directly. While Emmy could be rigid about sex, she still very much liked it and wanted to feel Marc's desire for her. So, it was distressing that he didn't initiate more often.

Learning about the pornography was quite devastating for Emmy because it confirmed her fear that she wasn't attractive enough for Marc—a worry she'd been unable to meaningfully address with him for fear of the answer. In fact, until the disclosure, Emmy had colluded in staying blind to her husband—especially the parts of him that didn't align with her wishes or desire for certainty. She craved predictability in the relationship to manage her challenges with anxiety, so she instinctively resisted acknowledging the full complexity of her husband's inner world.

The pornography didn't just shake her sense of self—it also left her disoriented, as the unspoken rules she had relied on were no longer working. Despite being attractive, chaste, obedient to church standards, and supportive of her husband in his calling and career—all the qualities she had been told would secure her a worthy spouse—she was married to a man who nonetheless chose pornography over her. She had believed that by adhering to these feminine roles and ideals, she could expect spiritual leadership, love, and security from her husband. Instead, she was left questioning the very principles that had once seemed so certain.

Marc had internalized these same gender expectations, and took on the role of the protective, benevolent priesthood holder as he believed he should. In fact, he actively kept this picture alive in his wife's mind because it mattered to him to be seen this way. And although he didn't think of himself as deceptive, masking his sexual mind along with his unorthodox beliefs was almost second nature. Years of practice had taught him how to conceal the unacceptable parts of himself—from his parents, his bishop, and even himself. But hiding these things from his wife—his intimate partner—pushed the marriage into crisis, shaking the very foundation of their relationship.

ROLE-PLAYING IN LDS MARRIAGES

Marc and Emmy's story is that of two people hiding from each other—a story of a couple playing house. It is not unusual. Many LDS couples enact the learned dispositions and duties of husband and wife while limiting how deeply they really know each other. Until their crisis, Marc and Emmy had colluded in limiting the transparency of their partnership, hiding behind the gender roles and mutual dependencies they had inherited.

One of the meanings operating at the foundation of Marc and Emmy's marriage was the inherited idea that wives are subject to their husbands. Woman comes from the rib of Adam, they learned, and was created to be his support and dependent. The Family Proclamation reinforced the understanding that men preside, provide, and protect. And church talks also shaped Marc's understanding of his role. For example, in April, 1998, President Hinckley taught the men of the Church, "The girl you marry will take a terrible chance on you. She will give her all to the young man she marries. He will largely determine the remainder of her life. She will even surrender her name to his name. As Adam declared in the Garden of Eden: 'This is now bone of my bones, and flesh of my flesh.'"

Like many church leaders, President Hinckley emphasized the inherent vulnerability of a woman choosing to bind her future to a man's. His message asked men to take seriously this responsibility. Yet embedded in the counsel is the assumption of women's intrinsic dependence and limited agency ("He will largely determine the remainder of her life"). Too often we honor women for their supposed innate virtue, but it is an honor based in the assumption of their limited power. In other words, women are often regarded as good because they are considered relatively impotent compared to men.

Albeit a product of President Hinckley's time, this messaging can reinforce a narrow characterization of femininity, and perhaps more importantly, can be taken as a divine sanction of women's submission to men's lives. Messages like these led Marc to see men's relationship to women as more parent-like than partner-like.

In fact, Marc remembered his Young Men leader quoting Elder Monson from general conference in October 1990: "[T]ears inevitably follow transgression. Men, take care not to make women weep, for God counts their tears." Such messages endeavor to warn boys about the harmful effects of sexual sin on a marriage. But Marc also interpreted them to mean that women are fragile and incapable of really knowing their husbands—sexually and otherwise. He told himself that a wife must be shielded from the world's darkness, but also in some measure, from the reality of her husband and his sexuality.

Marc's belief about the proper relationship between men and women reinforced—and justified—his inclination to mask his indiscretions. Telling himself he was protecting Emmy's innocence, he concealed many of his impulses, particularly those related to his sexuality. Of course, this protection was really for Marc—or more precisely, for the image he wanted to maintain. It also afforded him more latitude, since hiding his behaviors allowed him to avoid the deeper self-confrontation and responsibility that honesty would have demanded.

Though Emmy was distressed to learn of her husband's dishonesty, she had, in truth, participated in it by instinctively pressuring Marc not to disclose what she didn't want to see. While she had anxieties about the more inscrutable parts of him (such as his lower enthusiasm for sex and some indication of religious doubt), Emmy never asked for clarification. She didn't really want to know. When Marc brought up sincere perspectives that made her uncomfortable, she would either sharply criticize them or abruptly change the subject. This allowed Emmy to continue living within a limited picture of her husband and marriage without acknowledging her choice to be there. They both colluded in Marc keeping private what neither of them wanted to deal with.

Just like Adam and Eve in the Garden of Eden, Marc and Emmy retreated from the vulnerability of being seen. They used the fig leaves of their marital roles and culturally defined identities to cover their naked (honest) selves. In truth, they feared the humbling exposure of their shared humanity as well as the responsibility of choosing their lives in the face of it.

UNDER THE FIG LEAVES

Although many of us profess to want intimate connection, we are usually terrified to let a spouse see who we really are. Intimacy wakes us up to the humbling awareness of all the ways we fall short. Marc and Emmy were up against realities about themselves that were, in fact, *intimate*—and very uncomfortable.

The question for Marc and Emmy was whether they would use the crisis to acknowledge their respective contributions to the challenges in their marriage—or would they continue to hide in the form of self- and other-deception. The pornography issue at the crux of their crisis had within it information that could help them become stronger. And as we will continue to explore, if we are to become capable of an open-hearted relationship, we must endure the humbling exposures of "seeing [ourselves] through the unblinking eyes of . . . an honest spouse," as Michael Novak expresses in the quotation opening this chapter. To mature, to become more integrated and whole, we must tolerate knowing as we are known.

Part of what Marc and Emmy needed to wake up to was how deeply they depended on the other to feel like they were enough—and how each tried to manage that dependency through control. Marc exerted control by limiting his investment in the marriage. He kept much of himself hidden—masking his thoughts, desires, and behaviors, to control both how he was seen and what he might be asked to give. It also let him avoid reckoning with the real impact of his choices. He kept those choices out of his partner's line of sight so he could keep his justifications in place. Emmy sought control in a more direct way. She pushed Marc to do what would momentarily reassure her and ease her anxiety. She saw him, in many ways, as a buffer between herself and the world—and so she tried to manage how he moved through it.

NEEDING & BEING NEEDED: ONE-UP & ONE-DOWN VERSIONS OF CONTROL

One of the instinctive ways we express our dependency on others for a sense of self is in the creation of hierarchical relationships—relationships that allow us to extract security and validation from the person (ostensibly) below or above us. In our desire for *validation*, which is to say our pursuit of approval, we create relationships in which one partner's desires and priorities take precedence over those of the other. We seek validation by yielding to others' expectations or beliefs (as Marc often did with Emmy) or by pressuring others to yield to ours (as Emmy often did with Marc).

Emmy's dependency on validation was perhaps the most obvious: She had learned to understand herself as less capable than Marc. Growing up, her parents encouraged her to "be nice" and interact with others in non-threatening ways. They discouraged Emmy from pursuing a career or even working when she was single. This "wasn't feminine," they said.

104

Emmy learned that to depend upon a man was to be the kind of woman God wanted her to be. It was also the kind of woman men would find the most desirable. By suppressing herself, Emmy could make a man feel needed—"strong" by comparison—and by doing so, secure her place in his life. It also allowed her to sidestep the full responsibility of adulthood, something that felt overwhelming to her. When Emmy married, she was not so much looking for a *partner—an equal*—as she was looking for someone to look after her, just as she had been taught to expect.

In short, Emmy occupied a *one-down* stance relative to her husband. Not because she, in fact, had less potential, but because this was a disposition, a way of relating to herself and others, that was approved of—*validated*. She also took seriously the belief that her husband, a priesthood holder, was the family's spiritual leader and economic provider. While seeing Marc as stronger distorted her view of herself (and him), she preferred the idea of his protection. This was a socially validated use of him, and as long as he was enacting his half of the arrangement, she could stay blind to him as a whole person and blind to her responsibility to love him as a flawed, unique soul.

While Emmy looked to Marc for emotional and sexual validation (and confused this with desire), she was in no position to truly desire Marc. She wanted to be wanted—she wanted the security and validation that it afforded—but she didn't want to know her husband, especially when it interfered with her sense of security.

Needing & Being Needed: One-up & One-down Versions of Control

Marc may have looked like the stronger, more independent partner, but he *needed to be needed*—which is its own form of neediness. His sense of worth depended on Emmy seeing him as valuable. In fact, Marc had always been drawn to women who were dependent, feeling most secure when he was with someone who looked up to him. If Emmy depended on him, she wouldn't leave him, he intuited, and as the one providing the care, he would also have more control.

Even though Marc sought security through Emmy's dependence on him, there was nothing truly secure about their arrangement. Hierarchical marriages express a couples' psychological dependency on each other, and this makes the marriage vulnerable. The need for the other's approval and support will always compromise the authenticity and freedom in the marriage. It artificially diminishes the strengths in one partner while masking the humanity and fallibility in the other. This dependency also makes partners feel invariably controlled by the autonomy and invalidating differences of the other. All of this builds resentment, which erodes the happiness and stability of the marriage.

OUR CULTURAL MODEL OF MARRIAGE
IS VERTICAL & DEPENDENT

Although hierarchical marriages are fragile, we have generally reinforced them as our ideal. While we deeply value marriage, we do not explicitly value *intimate* marriage. Instead, we tend to focus instruction on the distinct roles and dispositions of men and women, including the idea that men should preside over their wives and families. In this hierarchical and role-based understanding, couples are encouraged to "serve one another" and "put the needs of the other first." This parallel and cooperative model is very different than the ideal of collaboration and intimacy, or the ability for partners to know and care for each other as equal, distinct individuals.

Marriage has served many functions throughout time and across cultures, most of which are unsentimental. Our Latter-day Saint pragmatic ideals for marriage are no different. We care about couples creating families and doing their part to "build up the kingdom." But many of us anticipate intimate partnership when we marry, not realizing that the way we think about marriage interferes with creating it. This is not to say that traditional roles are a problem or that men and women may not naturally gravitate toward different responsibilities in family life. But to the degree that our prescribed gender roles interfere with knowing ourselves, and to the extent that fulfilling them becomes the focus and measure of a marriage, we limit our capacity to create honest, soulful partnerships.

Of course, every culture defines for itself what it means to be male and female, but our LDS gender instruction tells us who *God* thinks we should be. Because we often consider these roles divinely ordained, we may too easily dismiss our individuality and personal responsibility in choosing our own path. Our deep desire for approval and belonging can pressure us to conform to group expectations—even at the cost of self-knowledge and being true to ourselves.

I certainly felt this pressure during my college years in the late 80s and early 90s—a time when church teachings strongly emphasized that women should not allow career aspirations to interfere with marriage and motherhood. Trusting that this was the faithful choice, most of my friends chose marriage over completing their degrees. I, on the other hand, turned down the opportunity to marry and pursued graduate school instead. In doing so, I faced the disapproval of those I desired approval from. Though I trusted God was not disappointed in my choice, it was challenging to stay true to myself when important voices framed my decision as inherently selfish—that pursuing education when marriage was an option was a betrayal of what mattered most.

When we pressure conformity to social expectations while calling this conformity "obedience," we obscure not just the importance of our God-given agency, we also weaken the self-knowledge and self-trust that agency fosters. These qualities (self-knowledge and self-trust) are essential to both our spiritual growth and our capacity to form intimate, meaningful relationships—an idea we'll explore further in the chapters ahead.

I want to emphasize that it is normal to approach love and marriage initially with the goal of getting our needs met. Pop songs, for example, constantly equate romantic love with need: *"Baby, I need you!"* is a common refrain. While this is typical, we work against intimacy and desire when we make mutual need-fulfillment the defining measure of a marriage, and equivalent to love. And although cultural instructions to "serve one another's needs" can give us a valuable starting point, idealizing this mutual dependency will limit our growth towards intimate, open-hearted partnership.

SEXUAL VALIDATION VS. SEXUAL INTIMACY

The human desire for validation often shows up most clearly in our sexual relationships. Because sex is so personal, it's natural to look to a spouse to affirm the part of us that feels the most vulnerable. But when our cultural messaging frames sex as a way to meet a spouse's *needs,* it gets in the way of developing and sustaining intimate desire. Church teachings about meeting one another's needs strive to teach conscientiousness in an intimate part of marriage, and this is important. But if we take it to mean that sex is an actual need that must be fulfilled, as many of my clients do, we undermine the sense of freedom and choice that marital intimacy thrives on.

My client Olivia lived very much in this understanding of sex: "Before I even got married, I understood that my husband's job would be to provide for us [financially] and my job would be to take care of everything else, including his sexual needs. And I really did understand them as needs—*needs that had to be fulfilled one way or another*. If they were not fulfilled by me, then he might fulfill them in some other way—like masturbation, pornography, or worse—an affair."

In this role-based, need-fulfillment understanding of marital sex, Olivia saw her marriage through a transactional lens, with each providing a service for the other. Olivia continued, "I also believed if I took care of [his] needs, he wouldn't leave me. He would need me too much to go anywhere else." As reassuring as the idea of mutual dependency can be in the vulnerability of intimate love, it doesn't give us what most of us hope for in marriage, which is to be *desired*—to be chosen for who we are. And the experience of choosing and being chosen in return is at the heart of intimate, passionate sex—and is very different from a role-based view of satisfying sexual needs out of duty.

The more we rely on a spouse to take care of us, whether sexually, emotionally, or economically, the less freedom we have to actually *choose* them. If, like Marc and Emmy, we need a spouse to prop up our sense of self—if we need them to show us we are enough—we are not yet in a position to desire—not yet able to *choose* them as they are. Marc, for example, needed Emmy to be something for him, which meant he could not desire her—not all of her. Role-playing in Marriage He wanted only the parts that made him feel strong and secure. He could not choose her as a whole person. He couldn't desire her apart from the role she played in supporting his sense of self. Such a feeling isn't real desire. It's the pursuit of validation in the name of desire. When we need approval, we don't have the psychological independence that a whole-hearted and intimate marriage requires.

Let me reiterate that it's common—both in and out of the church—for marriages to start out in this psychological dependency. But when we treat dependency as our ideal, we limit the erotic energy that intimate marriages thrive on. What is more, we interfere with what our marriages can become. Plenty of couples get through the act of sex, but far fewer are able to create sex that is soulful—born of true peace in one's skin and desire for the entirety of the other.

The truth is, most of us struggle to fully desire the soul of another—and to offer our own heart in return. Many go to great lengths to limit the vulnerability and investment that marriage calls us toward. Driven by fear of rejection and a need for control, we guard our hearts—even in sex—seeking refuge in more superficial partnerships, even as our souls ache to know and be known, to experience a marriage that is more authentic and life-giving.

INTIMACY, INVALIDATION, & GROWTH

Marc and Emmy began their marriage occupying roles relative to one another that allowed them to feel valued and secure. And in the beginning, that felt good. They each found a sense of worth and validation through the other. But over time, their dependent dynamic began to crumble under the pressure of reality. Intimacy—*truth*—was interfering with the stability of their marriage and pushing Marc and Emmy into crisis.

Their marriage wasn't in crisis *because* of the pornography; the crisis of pornography was revealing the marriage. Its revelations, as painful as they were, were putting them up against important developmental dilemmas—choices that are inherent to marriage and essential to each partner's growth. Much like Adam and Eve, life was asking Marc and Emmy to use their agency and define themselves in the world—to assert who they would be without any guarantee and without reassurance. In order to develop, they had to *self*-define, and that always requires exposure and uncertainty.

Much like Adam, Marc wanted two things that didn't go together: He wanted his wife to trust him, and he wanted to be invulnerable in the relationship. Since intimacy (truth) had revealed Marc's untrustworthiness, he could no longer have it both ways. He was at a crossroads. Would he choose the vulnerability it takes to be fully honest? Or would he remain masked and choose the supposed protection of staying distant (while sacrificing his wife's happiness)?

Like Eve, Emmy also desired two things that didn't go together: She wanted to keep depending on Marc for a sense of security, and she wanted to trust her own judgment and have honest confidence in herself. The first option interfered with the possibility of the second because it required her self-deception. She, too, had a decision to make: take the brave step of waking up and building honest self-trust, or depend on Marc while continuing to try and control him.

In the end, Marc and Emmy each stepped back under the fig leaves of their culturally validated identities—both too afraid of the exposures and risks of deeper honesty and personal responsibility. Afraid of what they couldn't control and the approval they might not get, they each chose what appeared to be safer, more validated paths while compromising their growth and the intimacy of the marriage in the process.

For Emmy this meant continuing to pressure Marc to be what she wanted rather than know him as he was—pressing him to go to a local sex addiction program, which she hoped would make him a man she could depend on again. He mostly complied with her desire (while lacking personal conviction that it was needed), while Emmy attended an online group for survivors of betrayal trauma (where she found easy validation for her plight).

While support groups *can* encourage deeper clarity and integrity, Marc and Emmy used theirs to reinforce their powerlessness and resentments. They claimed to be "working on the marriage" while in truth, they wanted validation more than growth. Marc and Emmy each placed responsibility for change outside of themselves and deepened the parallel nature of their lives. As a result, the marriage did not grow, but their resentments and loneliness did.

INTIMACY REQUIRES COURAGE

In the past few chapters, we've explored cultural messages about marriage and sex that undermine our capacity for intimacy. These messages of parents and teachers aren't intended to harm. They are instead a reflection of our collective entrapment in false traditions—traditions that veil the richness and beauty of our revealed theology. It's easy to internalize these limiting beliefs. Intimacy can be frightening, and both love and responsibility stretch us beyond what's comfortable. It is understandable that we often shrink from the potential for soul development and retreat into dependency and resentment instead.

Still, we can invite more beauty and eros into our lives if we're willing to endure discomfort, and trust in the power of truth and love. Our theology offers a meaningful path to growth, but the virtues that lead us there—faith and repentance, integrity and compassion—demand honesty and courage. Like Emmy and Marc, many of us resist the soul-stretching uncertainty that intimacy, agency, and transformation require. But in the pages ahead, through the story of another couple facing struggles similar to Marc and Emmy's, we'll explore how gospel truths help us grow in our capacity for joyful, intimate partnerships.

CHAPTER 4: SELF-REFLECTION QUESTIONS

We seek validation by either yielding to others'
expectations or by pressuring others to yield to ours.

1. Consider situations in which you conform to others'
   expectations even if they are counter to your own
   desires or sense of what is fair. Are there times when
   you conform against your better judgment to keep
   the ostensible peace?

2. If you do go against what you believe is best, why
   do you do it? What is your goal in yielding or
   accommodating?

3. What impact does this choice have on your feelings
   in the relationship? What impact does it have on your
   feelings about yourself?

----

4. What are ways that you pressure others to conform to your demands, anxieties, or view of the world? How do you exert this pressure? (Do you use intellectual arguments, act hurt, criticize, guilt the other person?)

5. Why do you do this? What is your goal?

6. What impact does this have on your relationship to your spouse? To others? To yourself? (e.g. How do they see you? How open are they to you? Do they trust you?)

7. What is your fear in allowing a spouse or important other to make their own choices?

_____

_____

_____

_____

_____

_____

_____

_____

_____

_____

_____

QUESTIONS CONTINUED

8. Considering the ways you seek validation in your marriage, can you see ways that this pursuit impacts the freedom or peace in your relationship? Can you see how it might impact desire and openness in your sexual relationship?

9. Reflecting on the ways you pursue validation, what might be stronger or kinder ways to handle these areas of invalidation / difference? What do you need to change to be more fair to your spouse? What do you need to address to increase your self-respect in the relationship?

I recommend going through these questions on your own at first, then going through them with your spouse. You will likely benefit from the perspective of a spouse or trusted loved one to expand your understanding of yourself and the ways you pursue validation.

INTIMACY BEYOND VALIDATION

5

"Sin happens whenever we refuse to keep growing."
—Saint Bradley of Nyssa

BEAMS, MOTES, & MISERY IN MARRIAGE

Couples reach out to me when their patterns of relating are no longer working for them—when their intimate struggles are undermining their faith in marriage and each other. In their distress, couples usually recognize that they are out of their depth—that the way they've made sense of their troubles is interfering with finding a way forward. They are stuck. At these impasses—when the emotional stakes are highest—couples are usually their most receptive to a new perspective on their marriage and themselves. They are often most open to uncomfortable information if it will help them untangle the knot of pain that has come to define the relationship.

"We no longer connect," is a common presenting concern, and one that reflects the quiet frustration of many couples. The sense of disconnection rarely stems from one catastrophic event; more often, it's the result of a slow erosion over time—small moments of unkindness, unspoken resentments, and missed opportunities to really listen. To help couples find their way back to each other, I look for the *behaviors* that are undermining the marriage. What, precisely, is each person doing—or not doing—that weakens the ease of connection they are longing for?

Many of us imagine that our contributions to a struggling relationship would be obvious. This is often not the case. We are remarkably skilled at justifying ourselves, telling palatable yet limited stories about our motives that blind us to our own role in the problem. "I am only defensive because you keep hammering on about this!" one partner might insist. "Well, I have to keep bringing it up because you refuse to listen!" the other retorts. These are the words of a couple caught in a power struggle—each focused on the other's shortcomings, unable to see or take responsibility for their part in a larger, painful pattern.

When we don't get the validation we crave, when our desires or perspectives are dismissed, our lesser selves tend to emerge. And our lesser selves—our *egos*—are notoriously poor at collaboration. The ego wants control, and in our effort to get it, we become less self-aware, less capable of listening, and less willing to face our part in a problem. In fact, how we handle ourselves when we are *not* getting what we want—how we navigate those moments of disappointment or frustration—determines the resilience of a marriage and whether it will grow or wither.

So, when couples come to me for help, my goal is to illuminate how their reactive, regressive behaviors are negatively impacting the marriage—how their "natural man" responses are undermining the intimacy and happiness they long for. What our behavior reveals about us is often hard to face; it challenges our self-perceptions and the stories we tell ourselves about who we are. It also exposes our hypocrisies—the contradiction between our ideals and our behavior.

As Christ taught in the Sermon on the Mount, our hypocrisies are like beams in our eyes—blind spots that distort our perception of the truth. These "beams" keep us from seeing how we contribute to the pain in our relationships. Of course, it is quite easy to spot the mote in our partner's eye. *Their* flaws, *their* blind spots, can be so obvious to us. But when we fixate on a spouse's shortcomings while ignoring our own, we keep ourselves from the information we need to become a better friend.

While we may be blind to ourselves, a spouse *can* see our negative contributions to the relationship. They live in the consequences of them (as we live in the consequences of theirs). Of course, they have blind spots of their own, but we often use what they get wrong about us to dismiss what they get right about us. This, of course, is our spiritual and relational vulnerability—the resistance to seeing ourselves *as we actually are*—to knowing ourselves as we are known. And because we cannot change what we cannot see, if we won't open our hearts to the truth that others are privy to, we are doomed to stay stuck in our dependency on others, doomed to keep hurting the ones we love.

This was the case with Hugh and Eloise, a couple who had been struggling in a desire discrepancy for several years when they reached out to me for help. Hugh wanted more frequency and variety in their lovemaking, but he generally kept quiet about his desires given his wife's guardedness around sex. Because Hugh had occasionally viewed porn prior to marriage, Eloise was motivated to keep the eroticism of their encounters relatively subdued. She was afraid if they ventured outside of their typical pattern (Sunday night sex that included about ten minutes of foreplay followed by missionary position intercourse usually ending in only Hugh's orgasm), it might awaken desires in Hugh that would take him (or them) in the wrong direction. Eloise didn't want to compromise the spirituality that anchored her life, and she felt that allowing more eroticism was risky. She feared the loss of control—over Hugh, over their relationship, and even how she experienced herself. So, although she didn't like to disappoint, she didn't want their intimate encounters to get *too* intimate.

Hugh reached out for an appointment after his wife discovered him looking at porn late one night. She had awoken to find him on his phone, watching a man perform oral sex on a woman—a sexual act that had been the subject of several conversations between them, and one that Eloise had made clear she had no interest in experiencing. Given

Eloise's rejection of the idea, Hugh had stopped bringing it up and sometimes channeled his frustration at Eloise's rigidity and anxiety through secretive porn viewing.

"I think Hugh has an addiction," Eloise announced within the first few minutes of meeting me. "Hugh led me to believe he'd overcome his porn habit when he was a teenager, but he admitted yesterday that he's continued to view it off and on since we got married almost three years ago."

In a faith culture steeped in anxiety about eroticism, a concept like "porn addiction" was not only a ready-made label for Eloise to explain her husband's disappointing behavior, it was a diagnosis she intuitively preferred. If Hugh's sexuality were fully pathological, she could ask him to change without having to look at any of her own difficulties with sex and intimacy. It allowed her to avoid acknowledging any role she might have in the issues emerging in their young marriage.

The label provided a certain comfort for Hugh as well. By seeing himself as an addict, he could maintain some distance from his choices—viewing the pull of pornography as something happening *to* him, rather than a behavior he was actively choosing. "I lie sometimes *because of my addiction*," clients have explained to me. The reality was that both Hugh and Eloise were afraid to look honestly at themselves, their sexuality, and each other. It scared them. It also showed me why they were stuck: They were using the others' beams to remain blind to their own.

Hugh acknowledged in our initial conversations that he had indeed chosen not to be fully honest in the marriage. As much as he disliked seeing himself as deceptive, it remained true that lying, obscuring the truth about himself, was easier than revealing himself to his wife. He hated facing her disillusionment. He wanted control over how he was seen as well as control over how he saw himself. This made masking unflattering realities intuitive.

Hugh's mother had struggled with depression and self-doubt for most of his childhood. Watching her suffer, he learned to avoid doing anything that could add to her burden—afraid he could break the very person he depended upon. Hugh also saw his father come home after long workdays to take on most of the household responsibilities whenever Hugh's mother was in the midst of a depressive episode. Like Marc in the previous chapter, Hugh absorbed the idea that strong men take care of vulnerable women. So, he enacted that role readily, even though it meant concealing the parts of himself that didn't fit the image of a righteous, strong man.

As is true for many boys, when Hugh discovered pornography as a young adolescent, he experienced a freedom in the explicit pleasures of this online world. Although he felt ashamed for being drawn to it, stepping into private erotic pleasure felt good. He craved the momentary escape from the constrained role of a dutiful son, the few moments in which he could delight in a world free of obligation or judgment.

Of course, because Hugh believed that worthy boys and men resist this part of themselves, he feared that his interest in the erotic made him inferior to others and deficient in God's eyes. And though a part of him wanted to quit thinking about sex altogether, Hugh couldn't seem to let go of this private, pleasurable escape—however transitory and guilt-inducing it was. As an adolescent, he hadn't yet learned how to regulate his emotions and choose deliberately, so he vacillated between episodic indulgence and deliberate suppression.

Intimacy Beyond Validation

Even after Hugh married Eloise and had a relational focus for his sexuality, his wife's anxious response to anything other than their predictable sexual routine made it difficult for Hugh to be forthright. He knew his desire for more sexual playfulness and spontaneity distressed her. "You're never satisfied," she would often say in response to any suggestion for something new or when he expressed the wish that she initiate sex occasionally.

While Hugh had more self-control than he'd had as an adolescent and more ability to manage his emotions without turning to the indulgences of porn, he could still respond to the frustration he felt in their relationship by going to this easy outlet on occasion. Given that his wife struggled with self-doubt, he told himself it was okay to mask his occasional missteps. If it kept Eloise from unnecessary distress, it was tolerable, even if not ideal, he reasoned.

While he valued seeing himself as a nice guy who prioritized his wife's happiness, Hugh also harbored quiet resentment for the love he didn't get in return for all his accommodations. As with many men, Hugh's caretaking came with an unspoken expectation: that it would earn him his wife's sexual accommodation, if not her desire. Like Hugh, many men feel resentment when their wives do not fulfill their side of this unarticulated bargain. For Hugh, this made it easier for him to indulge the idea that his private sexual behavior was justified, even that he deserved it, given the ways she did not give back to him. Hugh also knew the likelihood of sex would decrease if he were to be more forthcoming—that more honest intimacy would result in less sex.

So here they were, sitting in front of me trying to address topics they had become experts at avoiding. "Eloise is very anxious about sex," Hugh said uneasily, glancing over at his wife as if getting her permission to speak candidly. It was rare for them to talk openly about anything uncomfortable—especially something as vulnerable as sex—with a therapist listening in. As Eloise shifted awkwardly in her seat, Hugh continued carefully, "When I've said that I wish we could break from our routine, Eloise takes it hard. She wishes I were happy with how things are," he explained. "I don't want to upset her, so I don't bring things up much anymore."

"If you don't want me to be upset, then why are you willing to look at porn?" Eloise challenged. "You are doing things that make me feel insecure!"

Hugh could see the contradiction, of course. He'd told himself he wanted his wife to be happy, but his behavior clearly revealed this was not his only motivation.

"I know what you're saying. I've felt bad about it," Hugh said.

"Well, obviously not bad enough if you've kept doing it. I wish you'd just be more honest with me. How am I supposed to trust you when you're hiding who you are—doing things I have no idea about?" Eloise said, her voice thick with exasperation.

Hugh knew she was right about his untrust-worthiness and right that he had unfairly justified himself. So he attempted to address his justification. "But that's just it," he said. "You don't *really* want to know me in this way. The whole topic of sex stresses you out. You change the subject or complain whenever I bring it up. I already hate feeling like an imposition in general—but especially when it comes to sex. So I don't tell you things you don't want to hear," Hugh said.

Because Eloise knew this was truer that she wanted to admit, his statement stung.

"Hugh, what do you think would happen if you let yourself be more honest—if you revealed yourself more?" I asked.

Hugh had to think about this. There were two issues at the heart of my question: The first was the legitimacy of Hugh's sexual desires and behaviors. Were they worthy, or were they destructive? In wanting more playfulness and spontaneity, did Hugh desire something that would undermine them or strengthen them as a couple? Was he really interested in more aliveness—more eros—or was he just chasing things he had seen in porn, driven simply by his fear of missing out?

The second issue was the way Hugh was relating to Eloise as a partner. Was it really the job of a loving husband to "protect" his wife from reality—from knowing him? And who did the masking actually serve—Eloise or Hugh? Hugh used the idea that Eloise "can't handle the truth" as a way to avoid looking more squarely at *himself*. He also used this pseudo-protective identity to feel needed by his wife. Believing she depended upon him allowed him to sidestep the vulnerability of being known—and potentially not desired.

What's more, Hugh told himself that in accommodating his wife's desires and distress—in sacrificing his comfort for hers—he would earn her sexual desire and accommodation. And just like many men I work with, when this unspoken contract didn't pay off, Hugh's resentment at feeling used made it easy to justify his deception and indulgence. "I deserve something once in a while," he had thought to himself.

While Hugh masked the lesser parts of his mind to control how he was seen, his need to be needed also made it easy for Eloise to dismiss what she *did* understand about her husband's desires. His dependence on her approval and his discomfort openly claiming his desires gave her a great deal of implicit control. She could just "disapprove" of anything outside of her comfort zone, knowing her husband wouldn't push back. And in his scramble to be seen as good (which is not the same as doing good), he would accommodate, even as his resentment quietly grew.

If he was going to outgrow his dependency on Eloise's favorable opinion of him, Hugh needed more integrity—more alignment between his honest beliefs and his behavior. To do this, he had to confront whether his actions and preferences were indeed an obstacle to a better relationship—or if they were important to it.

The question was whether he should stand by his desires and choices with less apology or whether he ought to confront the lack of integrity in them and do better. By creating an honest alignment within himself—between his honest beliefs and his behaviors—he would become freer to *be himself*. He could be more knowable—and more able to know his wife—with less to hide and less to apologize for. But by having cultivated a hidden space, he had instead kept himself (and their marriage) from the growth they both needed.

As Hugh grappled with my questions, he acknowledged that he was conflicted. "I don't feel apologetic for my wish for more freedom in our relationship. Things can feel pretty controlled and flat

when we are together. It feels guarded and sometimes awkward. At the same time, I don't feel good
about the porn-viewing and the dishonesty—even
though it scares me to give up the porn entirely."

"Say more," I prompted.

"Well, to me, the porn feels indulgent—especially
the secrecy around it. I don't want to be a frustrated,
deceptive porn viewer. It's not a version of myself
I'm proud of. I'd feel ashamed if others knew about
it," Hugh confessed, pausing a moment to gather
his thoughts. "But what I am not clear about is how
to handle myself in this relationship. It's hard for me
that Eloise doesn't want to engage in a deeper way,
especially when it comes to sex. Sometimes I think
if I'm a good guy, I'll forget about the sex—but then
I get pretty mad about that, too," Hugh acknowledged. "I don't want to hurt her, but in all honesty,
a part of me feels taken advantage of and trapped—
like we always have to do things Eloise's way."

"Maybe porn has been a way you've tried to prove
that you're not trapped—that you are not controlled," I suggested.

Through our conversations, Hugh recognized
that sneaking had indeed given him an artificial
sense of freedom. Keeping parts of himself hidden
had seemed like the only way to navigate their relationship. To make Eloise feel good about him, he
had to hide his flaws; to make her feel good about
herself, he had to conceal his unhappiness. This
behavior not only made him feel bad about himself,
it made him feel bad about his wife, too. What's

more, his secrecy made it easy for her to distrust and discredit him—undermining the very ease and openness he claimed to want in the marriage.

His only way out of this trap was to grow—which meant becoming more honest and open, engaging with Eloise as an equal, and learning to tolerate what he couldn't control. But this kind of honesty, this way of relating to a woman, was unfamiliar to Hugh—and it scared him.

"Do you really believe Eloise is not strong enough to know you?" I asked, sensing his reluctance. "You don't think she can handle knowing your flaws or your desires?"

Hugh knew Eloise to be a very capable woman. She was an educated professional who had overcome significant challenges in her early life. In fact, part of the reason he was drawn to her was because she was more independent than his mother had been. Since he took relief in her autonomy, it surprised him that they were playing out a dynamic so similar to that of his parents'.

"I'm just uncomfortable pressuring her to do what I want. It seems mean," he stated.

"Perhaps masking your mind to keep her from making honest choices for herself is *meaner*," I suggested. "Listen, Eloise gets to decide who she's going to be in this marriage. Revealing who you are doesn't make her do anything—it doesn't harm her, even if it punctures an illusion or hope. In fact, letting her know you increases her ability to make choices she can truly stand by," I said. "It helps her grow into a person who is strong in her own right. This is far more respectful of Eloise than obscuring who you are to manipulate her perceptions and choices."

Eloise nodded in agreement with my challenge to her husband's duplicity. Yet, in reality, she was conflicted. She hated the idea of Hugh hiding his behaviors and beliefs from her, but at the same time, facing the truth about her husband—including his unhappiness—was daunting in its own right.

The less mature part of Eloise wanted Hugh to protect her from these choices—to reassure her that she was *desired* without having to *desire* in return, to take care of her, rather than ask her to be a full participant in their marriage. She was more comfortable with Hugh sticking his neck out, than risking vulnerability herself. In an anxious moment, Eloise shifted away from her *self*-confronting thoughts back to a reflexive, irritated focus on Hugh.

"What more do you want from me? We have sex at least once a week. Most husbands would be thrilled with that. It seems like whatever I do, it will never be enough for you."

Eloise regressed into a familiar rebuttal. Implying that Hugh wanted too much from her or that his sexual desires were excessive typically got him to back off his complaints into a conflicted silence. Also, making sex about a service she provided was a way to sidestep the question of her desire for Hugh—which was a far scarier question to address. But because Hugh was waking up to his participation in a less-than-honest, pseudo-protective relationship, he pushed himself to not retreat:

"I know I've focused on oral sex, and I make no apology for liking the idea of it. But your unwillingness to even consider the possibility is what bothers me the most. To me, it means your fears and anxieties will always run our marriage, and that really scares me. It's how things were with my mom and dad's marriage, and it's what makes me feel trapped sometimes. I don't want that for us. We started out with so much desire for each other. I miss that." Intimacy Beyond Validation

Hugh paused, bracing for the usual wave of defensiveness from Eloise—but instead his words lingered between them. Eloise *did* feel the impulse to bat this picture away. She wanted to tell Hugh that his words were hurtful—that they were unfair and made her feel small. But the sincerity in Hugh's voice struck her, and deep down she knew he was right. She had indeed pressured him to accommodate her insecurities rather than face them herself.

"I can understand why my anxieties around sex have been hard," Eloise acknowledged.

After a moment, Hugh replied thoughtfully, "What is actually hardest for me is feeling like you *put up* with me in sex. I don't care so much what we do together, I just really miss being wanted."

Eloise understood what Hugh was saying. She, too, missed the passion and excitement they once shared. But following their wedding, her natural desire had all but vanished—replaced by the sense that sex was now her duty, something expected of

133

her as a wife. (This sense of obligation was especially challenging to her desire given her pre-existing fear of having sex for the first time.) So once they were married, she pulled back, keeping Hugh at a distance and limiting the intimacy of their encounters. It just felt safer that way. She continued to want Hugh's attention, but she was afraid to truly open herself—to her sexuality and to him.

Although Hugh's honest feelings stirred regret in Eloise, becoming more sexual challenged everything she had been taught about how good women behave. She had learned that virtuous women don't dwell on their desires—that they approach sex with selflessness and restraint. If she were more sexual, would it undermine her life, her goodness? Would she become someone selfish and indulgent if she opened this door? She had watched her own mother refuse her father's affectionate overtures, batting him away with a covert superiority. And now, Eloise could see echoes of that same self-righteousness in herself. (She even felt the temptation to placate her husband with the oral sex he wanted—not as a gesture of connection, but as a way to keep her heart protected while appearing to try.)

Although Eloise had been taught that denying sex and pleasure was more virtuous, she recognized that it was ultimately a form of self-protection—and unfair to Hugh. She didn't want a marriage like her parents had, marked by long-standing resentments. Through our conversations, she came to see that the deeper issue was her fear of opening her soul and choosing to love Hugh fully. But out of integrity—and a genuine desire to grow—Eloise resolved not to let fear dictate her choices any longer. Choosing Hugh, rather than simply finding safety in being chosen, meant stepping into uncertainty. And so, she took that step and let down her self-protective wall.

Of course, stepping out from behind this wall of psychological girlhood required more than just the courage to love—it asked Eloise to make peace with her body and her sexuality, aspects of herself she had never truly explored or understood. While Eloise wasn't certain where this decision would take her, she felt the clarity that it was good. And even if it required some faith on her part, she believed she would be more whole for having chosen it.

We'll learn more about Hugh and Eloise's continued growth in the chapters that follow, but it is important to recognize that their change of heart immediately increased the eros energy between them. Couples fall more deeply in love and feel more alive when they love at the edge of their capacity—when they are willing to reach for what is better for the sake of love. Hugh and Eloise's courage resulted in deeper acceptance and joy between them as well as a more soulful kind of sex.

Hugh was surprised to find the draw of pornography diminish without much struggle. In coming to terms with himself and deciding honestly how he wanted to live, he felt more in control of his choices and saw less need to rebel against a perceived power outside of himself. Because his decisions were ones he respected, he also felt freer, even when exercising self-control. He found it progressively less tempting to indulge a pleasure that felt inferior to what he was experiencing in the marriage—a marriage that was becoming more honest and alive.

For Eloise, watching Hugh embody more integrity not only deepened her respect for him, but it increased her willingness to be open to him, too. His growing strength of character was attractive. And in choosing to lean in—out of a place of self-definition rather than obligation—Eloise felt more like herself in sex than ever before. Because discovering and developing her sexuality reflected her own desires, it no longer felt like she was losing herself in sex. She felt free even when doing something that asked more of her.

In fact, accepting her body and its capacity for pleasure was a way to know herself—a way to more deeply be herself. The more she accepted herself and her body, the more sex became a source of inner ease. And it was an ease that extended to Hugh as they began to create a sexual bond that was as good for Eloise as it was good for their relationship.

THE TRUTH SHALL MAKE YOU FREE

Eloise and Hugh's story illustrates how the exposures of an intimate relationship propel our personal growth if we will let them. When our conscience can no longer justify the ego-serving behaviors that our relationships reveal, *we change*. For Hugh, seeing himself through Eloise's eyes awakened him to his own superiority and dishonesty. Likewise, when Hugh revealed his deeper self to Eloise, she could no longer justify her self-righteous, guarded stance. As the scales fell from their eyes, they each felt a desire to become better—more aligned with what they knew in their hearts to be loving and fair. In choosing to listen to their consciences, they began to grow up—a growth that not only blessed their marriage, but enriched their individual souls as well.

Our capacity for personal and spiritual growth is directly tied to how much truth we are willing to integrate. An honest confrontation with our lesser selves always catalyzes repentance and character evolution. This important self-awareness can come from a perceptive therapist, a candid friend, or any wise observer who sees our blind spots more clearly than we do. But more often than not, that crucial observer is the one we share a bed with. An honest, invested spouse usually has a clearer view of our blind spots than we may want to admit.

My client Bentley confidently saw himself as the more evolved spouse in his marriage, coaching his wife Molly on how to live her life "better"— which, in his mind, meant becoming more like him. Convinced he was a step ahead in life, he endeavored to "lead Molly into her strength," a concept he had picked up from some of the masculinity-affirming podcasts he'd been listening to.

What Bentley failed to grasp was that the most blatant immaturity in the marriage was his own. His superiority was suffocating Molly even as he told himself her reluctance to yield was a sign of her own weakness. For all her quiet self-doubt, Molly could see what Bentley could not: her husband had little interest in knowing her—sexually or otherwise—unless it aligned with his interests and priorities. When she tried to share her honest perspectives, he dismissed them outright. Bentley's fear of losing his sense of superiority blinded him to the truth he most needed—the recognition that his own behavior was undermining the marriage he desired.

Like Bentley, most of us shy away from really knowing our spouses. To see them fully is to risk seeing ourselves. And even when unflattering information pierces through, we usually fend it off with self-justification. "You just don't get me. . ." we might say when an unflattering picture is reflected back to us. The "natural man" in all of us hates the exposures of being truly known. The ego has no interest in surrender.

Consider your own relationships. How do *you* resist seeing yourself and your negative impact? Do you punish your partner when they are honest with you? Do you tell yourself you are smarter or more righteous than your spouse so you don't have to consider seriously their point of view? Do you focus on the many ways you have been disappointed, so you can look away from the ways *you* disappoint? As with the couples we've read about in the previous pages, it's so easy to insulate ourselves from the truths we need; it is so intuitive to focus on anyone and anything but ourselves.

TO LOVE IS TO GROW

As we'll explore in the next two chapters, increasing our ability to love is central to God's plan for us. Love is precious precisely because it is *not* a given. It is not *natural*. The "natural man" seeks his own. Hugh and Eloise's choices were noble because they rose above the very human impulse to self-justify, to stay blind. Unlike Emmy and Marc of the previous chapter, they were willing to lose themselves, lose their egos, for the sake of love. And in doing so, they found themselves (see Matthew 10:39). In other words, they found a peace with themselves and with each other that their souls longed for. When asked which is the greatest commandment, Christ answered that it is to love each other. This is the central focus of our faith. It is by growing in our ability to love that we experience the joy our souls are capable of—the intimate communion (with God and with others) that we need to sustain ourselves in a world full of uncertainty and loss.

As you respond to the questions on the following page, I encourage you to be as honest with yourself as you can be. It is through your willingness to challenge your self-justifications that you can address your blind spots and grow beyond the impasses that limit your relationship. How brave will you be? Remember, "sin happens whenever we refuse to keep growing." The courage you bring to these questions speaks to your priorities—whether you're more focused on protecting your ego or committed to the growth that truth and love ask of us. Our choices reveal us.

Remember, while the truth can hurt at first, it ultimately sets us free. If you want to start having more productive conversations, consider stating forthrightly where your spouse is right about you rather than going on about where they are wrong. This will likely shift your marriage out of a power struggle into a more productive conversation, since more truth will be available to it. If your spouse is also willing to approach this conversation with honesty, you will be amazed at the power and potential you have to grow into a stronger, more intimate couple as you integrate more truth into your marriage.

CHAPTER 5: SELF-REFLECTION QUESTIONS

1. What are some of the (difficult) things you have come to understand about yourself through your marriage / spouse?

2. Have these insights shaped or changed your choices? If so, in what ways? (If not, why not?)

3. What impact has your willingness / unwillingness to change had on you? What impact has it had on your relationship?

4. What is something your spouse honestly believes or experiences with you that you have resisted accepting or been defensive about?

_____
_____
_____
_____
_____
_____
_____
_____
_____
_____
_____
_____

QUESTIONS CONTINUED

5. What kinds of behaviors have you engaged in to avoid acknowledging the truth in your spouse's perspective?

6. Even if you disagree with aspects of your spouse's point of view, what are they getting right about you?

7. What impact has your defensiveness or resistance had on your marriage? What behavior does your unwillingness to self-confront invite from your spouse?

----

8. Are there truths that the marriage needs that you have been reluctant to reveal? If so, what are they? What are you afraid would happen if you were to speak more honestly?

9. In what ways will you bring more self-exposure / intimacy into your marriage?

10. Where do you need to behave differently to have more alignment within yourself between what you value and what you are choosing?

CHANGING OUR MINDS

*"That which we most need will
be found where we least want to look."*
—Carl Jung

We change whenever our experiences cannot be accommodated by our current way of being in the world. The school of hard knocks pressures the reorganization of our minds to accommodate more reality. In the view of developmental psychologist Robert Kegan, maturation is not about adding knowledge to the fixed container of the mind. Instead, it is primarily about *transformation*, not just in terms of what we know but also the way we know—an evolution in how we make sense of the world around us. For example, as a teen I remember telling my friends how much I liked a movie I had seen at age eleven. When I watched it again as a young adult, I was chagrined to see juvenile humor, limited sophistication, and subpar acting. The content hadn't changed, but I certainly had. I had *changed my mind*. Similarly, when I revisited childhood books as a young adult, I read the same words yet understood the message of the book differently—from a different mind.

While reorganization of the mind is foundational to development, the process of changing our minds can be quite uncomfortable. Development is disorienting and disorganizing, especially at the onset. Because of this, it often feels as though things are going backwards when, in reality, they are moving forward. I watched my children struggle through this developmental process as they learned new cognitive or physical skills. My daughter, a violinist, had an engrained left-hand posture that needed to change. To grow in her musicianship, she needed to replace it with a new posture that at first felt very unnatural. Not only did the new position create awkwardness, it resulted in all of her other left-hand skills falling apart for a time. She couldn't shift with the same ease, her vibrato became more forced and her frustration was high. In the important process of changing her mind, it seemed as though she was losing skills. Of course, once she mastered the new hand position, her skills not only returned, but improved, and an entirely new level of playing capacity opened up to her. It was well worth her trouble, but the process required forbearance.

It is humbling and stressful for all of us when a previous way of thinking or behaving falls apart and we don't yet know a better way. Challenging false traditions, as we did in the earlier chapters of this book, can hurt. When we acknowledge the limitations of a previously accepted path, it can feel like we are destroying something precious and losing our way. But if we resist the disorientation that more truth brings, we undermine our progression. Truth really does "enlarge the soul" (Doctrine

& Covenants 121:42), but not without first stretching it beyond comfort.

Foundational to our spiritual and relational development is repentance. The Greek word for repentance—*metanoia*—literally means "to change one's mind." Changing our minds, *repenting*, requires not just the rupture of a current self-concept—it also requires tolerating uncertainty as we reach towards a better version of ourselves. Disillusionment with any foundational understanding of reality (including who we believe ourselves to be in that reality) can bring significant anguish.

A client of mine, highly invested in her identity as a "good mother," was seriously distressed when she woke up to the fact that she was encouraging her children's unhealthy dependence on her while unjustly alienating them from their father. Although it was painful to confront the unfairness of her behavior, that bitter realization was critical to doing right by her children. Tolerating the puncture to her self-concept was a necessary step in becoming the kind of mother she truly aspired to be. As Kegan articulates, "Grief, mourning, and loss" are "the dying of a way of knowing the world which no longer works, a loss of an old coherence with no new coherence immediately present to take its place."[1]

Because the death "of a [familiar] way of knowing the world" can feel deeply unsettling, we instinctively resist it. One common defense is to reject information that doesn't fit easily into our current worldview. This might look like only consuming news sources that confirm our beliefs, reacting defensively when our spouse challenges our perspective, or rationalizing away insights that threaten our sense of self. We may claim that "communication problems" are at the root of our marital conflicts, but more often, the issue is not that our spouse doesn't understand us—it's that they understand us all too well, in ways we're not yet prepared to accommodate.

To stabilize our way of knowing the world, we instinctively create meanings that make sense to our current mind (such as "he doesn't speak my love language" or "she is too sensitive") while obscuring the information our souls and marriages need to grow. (What did you learn about the ways you avoid accepting the truths your spouse is revealing to you? See the self-reflection questions at the end of chapter 5.) As you may see in your own behavior, most of us don't want to endure a truth-based reorganization of who we are, even though our avoidance costs us our strength.

Richard Rohr, a Catholic priest, teacher, and prolific writer, discusses the crisis of meaning and self-understanding that is essential to our spiritual development. In his book *Falling Upward*, he characterizes a "fall" as so central to human character development that it can be found everywhere in literature and scripture. The creation story is a narrative that includes not only a fall from grace,

but a fall from innocence into complexity. ☞
As Rohr teaches, falling is a divine pattern that
hides in plain sight because we don't want to see it.
We prefer the idea that obedience will earn us favor
and protect us from loss and struggle—something
we have in common with the brother of the prodi-
gal son in Christ's parable.

While choosing wisely will indeed avert some
regret and unnecessary suffering, we can't escape
the fact that life will challenge and expose our
limitations. As much as we understand the importance of "choosing the right," the truth is, we often
grow much more by doing things "wrong" than by
doing them "right."

Looking back, I recognize that it was during the
most painful chapters—when life was *not* working
as desired—that I grew the most. As a teenager, I
struggled to fit in with my peers. Despite my
efforts to be well-liked, I found little of the acceptance I longed for. Though it was difficult, it was
the absence of approval that became the catalyst to
seeking a deeper source of strength: my relationship with myself and God. The self-knowledge and
self-acceptance that emerged made me stronger

☞ Richard Rohr and other developmental theorists view the shift from
    simplicity to complexity as a necessary stage of growth, not a failure
    of faith. What feels like a fall—into doubt, contradiction, or ambigu-
    ity—is often the beginning of growth and transformation. Mature
    faith doesn't cling to certainty but learns to hold paradox and
    mystery. In this way, complexity becomes a sign that true spiritual
    and personal development is underway.

and set me on a more meaningful path. Though I still prefer the comfort of validation, I recognize that growth comes when I'm pushed beyond my current capacity or humbled out of a limited understanding.

This illustrates the moral virtue and transformative power of humility. The discomfort I once resisted was actually the doorway to a different kind of strength—not one built on control or certainty, but on humility. Humility is not about feeling *inferior*; it is about letting the truth matter more than our ego. It requires the courage to lose the self we know in order to grow into a more truthful understanding of who we are—including a clearer view of our relationship to others and to God.

As we saw in Hugh and Eloise's story, we must lose ourselves to find ourselves (Matthew 16:25). Some theorists refer to this process as "post-traumatic growth"[2]—the psychological development that emerges from struggle. Our minds and souls expand to accommodate more reality, becoming more capable of responding within greater complexity. As Einstein is purported to have said, "We cannot solve our problems with the same thinking we used to create them." Or as Kegan put it in *The Evolving Self*, "Any real resolution of [a] crisis must ultimately involve a new way of being in the world."[3] This is how we mature.

Soul development requires faith. Joseph Smith taught that faith is not just belief; it is a "principle of action."[4] To have faith is to trust sufficiently in the truth that we dare to act within it, even when clarity is limited and certainty is absent. In the previous chapter, we saw Hugh and Eloise embody this kind of faith. When they confronted their lesser selves, they each chose new action that aligned with what they believed to be more right—more loving. They acted without guarantees and without mastery of the new behaviors. Yet in both cases, their faithful actions led to deeper integrity with themselves and an expanded capacity to love.

DEVELOPMENT & THE CONTINENTAL DIVIDE

Several developmental theorists (including Jean Piaget, Lawrence Kohlberg, and Robert Kegan) have observed and defined the cognitive, moral, and relational progression of human beings. Interestingly, development in any one of these domains correlates strongly with development in the others—they seem to evolve concurrently. To characterize our development simply, we all begin in a state of egocentrism. At first, we make sense of the world by how it impacts us alone. (We are the center of reality as far as we are concerned.) But as we develop, we become progressively more able to see beyond our immediate experience, understanding ourselves and others from a broader vantage point. And as our perspective expands, we unlock higher levels of moral and spiritual reasoning that allow us to relate to ourselves and others with greater wisdom.

This growth happens in recognizable developmental stages. Some theorists define development in as few as two stages, others in as many as eleven. I have created a three-stage model that captures the

developmental phases I see most frequently in my clients. My model draws heavily on Kegan's developmental theory, but others (including Kohlberg, Piaget, and Fowler) have informed and inspired my thinking as well (see resources for further reading).

Before we learn about these three stages, a few thoughts to consider: You will see yourselves and others in these descriptions. As you do, keep in mind that we all start our journeys in STAGE 1. None of us gets a head start and there is no skipping ahead. We each work our way toward more advanced stages, with varying degrees of success. Remember that even as some of us become capable of more developed ways of thinking and relating, we all will regress to earlier mindsets with regularity. (Consider how you relate to yourself and others under stress versus when you are calm.) And lastly, we all tend to believe we are at a higher stage of development than we actually are, so beware of being too self-congratulatory. Understanding these stages helps us make sense of our behavior and provides a clearer map for the soul work we're undertaking.

STAGE 1: THE EGOCENTRIC STAGE

I call the first of the three developmental stages *egocentric*. This is the stage where we are necessarily self-centered, preoccupied with our own desires, and impulsive. Not yet able to comprehend the experience of others, nor regulate our impulses to manage our impact, our *feelings* largely dictate our choices and we view others in terms of how they serve *us*. This isn't to say that others do not matter to us at this stage—they do. But we are not yet capable of thinking beyond how others serve and affect us.

Since we have not yet learned how to make good choices, yielding to the authority of others is critical in our early lives. Knowing the world is bigger than we are, we obey to keep ourselves safe and to stay out of trouble. While we may choose not to lie during this stage, it is not (yet) because we are mindful of the impact lying would have on others. It is instead based on our effort to avoid any negative consequences for *ourselves*. To illustrate, when I was four years old, I wrote my name on the wall behind the couch. I knew it was not allowed, *but it felt so good to do it*. When my older brother asked me if I was the one who had written "Jennifer" (complete with a backwards J), my desire to avoid punishment prevailed: I told him that my two-year-old brother was the culprit. The impulse to lie was based on my concern for my own interests and safety, not on how it might impact my brothers or my relationship to them.

Most of us, with time, become capable of higher levels of moral and relational capacity, but a significant percentage of adults continue to function from this developmental position most of the time. To illustrate, my married client Will was compulsively unfaithful. He was also punishing and sulky when his wife, Eve, expressed her difficulty trusting him or acknowledged any unflattering aspect of him or his family of origin. "If I try to talk about the infidelity, he spirals and stops talking to me, so I just can't bring it up," Eve explained.

Will continually resisted any acknowledgment of the destructive impact the infidelity had had on his wife or their marriage and would instinctively shift the conversation to his own feelings instead. He was preoccupied with *his* hurt in the marriage and regarded these feelings as the justification for his disloyal behavior. In short, Will interpreted the world almost exclusively in terms of how it impacted him.

Will's mother and father, now divorced, were very similar. Both self-absorbed, they made their own feelings and impulses more important than their responsibility to their children. When Will's mother came to meet her first grandchild, she used the opportunity to announce her recent tryst with a married man. While her demand for the spotlight during such an important time was astonishing to Eve, it was far less so for Will. Knowing his mother well, he regarded this type of behavior as normal, expected even. Growing up in an environment where parents failed to model and hold consistent expectations of themselves or their kids, it was difficult for Will to organize his impulses and grow beyond his natural egocentrism.

Had Will grown up in a more secure and predictable home, he likely would have moved (sometime in pre-adolescence) into the next stage where we become more conscious of our relationship to and impact on others. This progression is not a repudiation of the first stage—our capacity to consider how our choices impact our safety will always be included and integrated into subsequent stages. These ego skills are foundational, even as new developmental capacity supersedes earlier mindsets. And although we may progress, we remain capable of regressing into earlier stages, particularly under stress or when in conflict with important others.

STAGE 2: THE SOCIAL STAGE

While our own individual feelings and impulses are primary in the egocentric stage, as we transition to the *social* stage our focus shifts toward the desire to belong. We begin to seek acceptance from our family, church, and broader community. In our effort to belong, we internalize and conform to the norms and beliefs of the groups we identify with. We are not yet able to truly think for ourselves at this stage, so our personal beliefs largely reflect the beliefs of our groups (even though it *feels* like they are our own).

In the social stage, we experience ourselves *as others experience us*. Highly attuned to how well we meet our group's expectations, our self-perception is more or less dictated by how others see us. We don't yet have a true *self*-reference. Accordingly, the thought "Dad loves me" in this stage becomes the self-concept of "I am loveable." Or "My teacher thinks I'm good at writing" becomes "I am a good writer." This social dependency is what psychologist David Schnarch refers to as a "reflected sense of self." In other words, our sense of self is embedded in our relationships and in what others mirror back to us. In this stage, we are not yet capable of true psychological autonomy, as our sense of self lives in other people.

Stage 2: The Social Stage

The social mind is similar to the egocentric one in that it is still preoccupied with the ego: *What is best for me?* continues to be a defining question. The difference is that the ego of the social mind is focused primarily on securing belonging. Someone in the social stage pays attention to how their behavior impacts the relationships they depend upon. So, we don't avoid lying in this stage simply to avoid getting into trouble; we avoid lying because we don't want to damage the relationships we need *and* we don't want to hurt those we care about. Self-interest is still involved but in a broader way than in the egocentric stage. We may be tempted to lie or conceal truths to protect our standing in the minds of others, but we also don't want to harm others' trust in us. How can I be truthful and also be accepted if who I am is different than what my group values? These are the tensions a person in the social stage grapples with.

MID-CHAPTER REFLECTION QUESTIONS

1. What are some ways that you try to manage how you are perceived by others?

2. What do you want or need others to believe about you? (Circle any that apply and add your own: *I care that others see me as* . . . hard-working, humble, loyal, self-effacing, funny, wealthy, self-sacrificing, powerful, intelligent, attractive, kind, brave, generous, thoughtful, creative, unique / unlike other people, righteous or spiritual, compassionate, someone worth listening to, someone worth cultivating a relationship with, etc.)

3. How do you try to show or *prove* you possess these qualities?

4. If others do not see you in this preferred way, how does it affect you?

5. When you let others' judgment determine your value, you continue to be dependent upon them. What is standing in the way of holding your sense of value more confidently within yourself? What might help you release the need to anchor your sense of self in how others perceive you?

Societal institutions facilitate our development into this stage. Institutions offer structure—rules and consequences—that help us regulate our impulses and choose in ways that benefit the functioning and purposes of the group. For example, in a ward we are given various callings and responsibilities. We are also offered principles and standards that represent what we collectively believe and value. These communal expectations help us grow beyond our impulsivity and self-preoccupation. They help us learn to cooperate with others. In this stage, we learn principles that are broader than any particular rule: "Do what is right, let the consequence follow" is one important example. Learning these rules of conduct and broader principles within a cohesive group is very important in facilitating the relational and spiritual capacities of STAGE 2.

As an example, when I was a missionary in Spain, we taught a man who struggled with alcoholism and under-employment. He resolved to stop drinking and joined the Church. He was eventually given a calling, which helped him find a sense of purpose and belonging in a community that cared about him. By striving to follow the standards of the Church in that supportive environment, he became a more responsible father and husband, and a more capable human being overall. His family felt better about him, and he felt better about himself as he became more able to manage his baser impulses. Like all who develop into the social stage, he was moving out of impulsivity into a mind capable of responding to the needs and expectations of his family and community. Benefiting from the institutional expectations of the Church, he grew into a man who was *response*-able.

STAGE 3: THE SELF-AUTHORING STAGE

While the majority of adults spend most of their lives primarily in **STAGE 2**, a few courageous souls make the qualitative shift in thinking that is required of the *self-authoring* mind (**STAGE 3**). The shift from being socially driven to being personally directed is so significant that LDS therapist Marybeth Raynes called it "the continental divide" in human development."[5] Crossing the continental divide from a socially embedded self to a more differentiated and personally determined one requires a radical shift from external validation and authority (What do others expect of me?) to internal validation and authority (What do I expect of myself?). Someone in the self-authoring stage chooses not to lie not only to avoid hurting someone they care about, but also because lying violates their own conscience. Put differently, lying conflicts with what they expect of themselves.

Although the self-authoring stage becomes cognitively possible in late adolescence, few of us tolerate the exposure, personal responsibility, and potential social invalidation that comes with this stage. So, while almost all of us will identify with and embody aspects of **STAGE 3**, most people live their lives primarily in the validation pursuit of **STAGE 2**. It's important to note that the path to higher stages is not linear and no one arrives at the self-authoring stage to permanently reside there. It usually looks like two steps forward and one step back—functioning at higher stages under some circumstances while regressing to lower stages in others. Even when we're capable of self-authoring, under enough relational pressure, fear, or emotional exhaustion, we can temporarily regress into the approval-seeking of **STAGE 2** or even the black-and-white thinking of **STAGE 1**.

Recall that when we are in **STAGE 2**, we internalize the norms of our group and hone the awareness of our impact on others. But as we transition into the self-authoring stage, we become less dependent on others to tell us how to think and who to be. Instead, we start sorting out what we believe and who we are in relation to these inherited values. Our thinking also becomes more flexible as we discern what's right and wrong in any given situation. In confronting the complexity of life's choices, we begin to focus not just on the letter of the law but on the spirit of it, too.

To be clear, self-direction in this stage is not a *rejection* of external authority. In fact, defining a self through any reactive defiance of external expectations is just another form of dependency on authority. (One depends on convention to know what to rebel against.) Self-authoring is also not indifference to others' feelings, nor is it *anti*-dependent (as in, the refusal to benefit from others' help or presence in our lives). Instead, self-authoring is the ability to reference the conscience we have been developing through the cognitive and moral work of stages 1 and 2—a conscience that helps us assess what is needed, determine who we are in relation to that need, and act on what we believe is right, even when the cost is great.

Given the lessened dependency on social approval, the ability to love others actually increases in this stage. We no longer love in pursuit of security (STAGE 1 love) or belonging (STAGE 2 love). Instead, we love from the desire to do what is right by another. In other words, we love for its own sake rather than to address the needs of the ego. In short, the right hand doesn't know what the left hand is doing. Less in need of recognition or praise, we become more capable of godly love.

The ability to self-author—to shift the locus of authority from the outside to the inside—also deepens our capacity for intimacy. No longer driven by the need for approval, we are freer to share our thoughts, perceptions, and hearts with openness and integrity. This freedom enriches marriage, where we can more fully offer not only our minds and emotions, but our sexuality as well.

At this stage, we become more capable of truly knowing and investing in others—even when it means facing their dissatisfaction with us, or encountering values and desires that differ from our own. Guided by integrity rather than validation, we learn to tolerate, and even make use of, moments of invalidation. The intimacy of our relationships becomes a place where we bring our values into greater alignment with reality—where belief and behavior can meet with honesty.

In the self-authoring stage we are finally more able to desire another soul. We'll talk more about desire and its connection to **STAGE 3** self-definition in the next two chapters. But for now, it's enough to say this: with less need for approval, we are more capable of desiring another soul and bringing our whole selves to that choice. Less driven by ego, we are more able to see their inherent beauty and to share ourselves with an open heart.

KATIE & ERIC TRAVERSE
THE CONTINENTAL DIVIDE

It is difficult to let go of the validation pursuit that defines **STAGE 2**. Our deep desire to belong makes it challenging to tolerate the exposure and risk of differentiating from our group and taking deeper responsibility onto ourselves. As a result, we usually don't cross the continental divide into a stronger internal authority until sufficient pressure pushes us. This pressure often emerges when the values we've inherited come into conflict with each other— when life presents dilemmas that make it impossible to get the validation we desire while doing what we believe is most right.

As the story of Adam and Eve teaches us, asserting choices within competing desires and moral positions is fertile ground for soul development. Put differently, we grow in our spiritual capacity as we choose for ourselves which moral position we will stand behind. This doesn't result in getting everything we want, but it does lead to greater internal strength and a deeper ability to be a force for good in an imperfect world.

The story of Eric and Katie from chapter 1 offers a clear example of the transition from **STAGE 2** to **STAGE 3**, and how that shift can expand a person's capacity for intimacy. During the social stage, Eric had internalized the value that commitment to marriage and family is important. He also grew up learning that he should treat his wife fairly. On top of this, he valued a sexually intimate marriage— something he had experienced in his first marriage and hoped to share with Katie.

The problem was that Katie did not like sex and didn't want the exposure of it. Given that they'd worked on their relationship with me for several months to little effect, Eric was facing the fact that his wife didn't desire a sexually intimate marriage. This put him at an impasse. His values were in conflict: He couldn't create a sexually intimate marriage and remain married to Katie. These were legitimate desires and values, but he could not have both in his current situation.

There was also no path that allowed Eric to keep everyone happy with him and still be at peace with himself: If he chose to leave the marriage, his family and community would judge him. But if he stayed only to keep others happy, would he betray himself? This internal conflict pressured Eric to self-define— to shift from an external reference point (*What do others expect of me?*) to a deeper internal one (*What do I expect of myself in this situation?*). To move beyond the impasse, he had to tolerate loss—of a false hope, of others' validation—and face the uncertainty about what his self-authoring choices might bring.

Back in chapter I, I described a meeting with Katie and Eric, where I told Katie I saw no real evidence that she wanted an intimate marriage—and pointed out to Eric that he was avoiding that hard reality. Eric had indeed been avoiding this self-defining moment by focusing on Katie—by hoping against evidence that she would come to want what he wanted. This moment in therapy marked a turning point for him. He began to accept the truth: Katie didn't want a sexual relationship with him. In admitting this to himself, he made a crucial shift: He let go of trying to control what he couldn't— his wife's desire—and focused instead on what he could—his own choices.

When they returned to see me two weeks later, Eric was far more grounded than he had been. No longer trying to shape Katie's choices, he spoke from a steadier place within himself: "I love you," he said. "But after a lot of thought, I've decided I need to let the issue of sex go. You don't want a sexual relationship, and although it breaks my heart, I've decided it's time to stop pressuring you to want something you don't truly want. We've worked with Jennifer for a while now with no real change, and I've decided I need to take your 'no' for an answer. I'm not going to leave—I'll finish raising the kids with you. And once they're grown, I'll see what the right path is at that point. But for now, I need to stop trying to make the marriage something that you don't want it to be."

As you may remember from chapter 1, Katie began our work by saying she'd be fine if she and Eric never had sex again—and at the time, she truly meant it. She didn't want the exposure and pressure of it. And with Eric in pursuit of her, she could get the validation of his desire without having to risk returning it. But now, confronting the loss of his energy and attention, Katie was waking up to herself. No longer in reaction to Eric's desires, she was beginning to sort out her own. It turned out, she didn't want a platonic relationship after all.

When next Katie returned with Eric, she had already started facing herself more honestly. She had spent the past two weeks thinking about the martyr energy that had shaped her life—a dynamic she'd inherited from her mother, who "gave" while feeling quietly superior, who accommodated while withholding her heart. Katie understood her fear in choosing to love Eric, but she couldn't respect the way she had let that fear shape her. She didn't like the version of herself she had become—and she knew she wanted to be braver.

Although it frightened her, Katie told Eric that she truly wanted the marriage—and that she wanted *him*. She preferred the uncertainty of a genuine sexual connection over the certainty of losing the erotic foundation that had once held them. And once she made that self-defining choice, what had long felt out of reach for her began to unfold with surprising ease. No longer resisting Eric, no longer at cross purposes within herself, Katie experienced her first orgasm just a few weeks later.

As we'll see in the chapters that follow, sexual desire thrives in freedom. Though on the surface it might look like Katie's turn toward Eric took her back to the same trapped place, it was different now, as she knew the choice was truly her own. It reflected her courage—a part of herself she respected. The more she lived in harmony with her conscience, the more she was becoming herself. And in that congruence, she felt a deeper freedom.

We cross the continental divide whenever we choose our *higher desires*—those grounded in integrity and conscience (eros choices)—over our *lesser desires*, those driven by validation, fear, or pride (thanatos choices). This moral progression is always facilitated by seeing ourselves more truthfully. It is also facilitated by conflict—conflict between competing values, conflict between our beliefs and our behaviors. As we assert our agency in those conflicts, determining the kind of lives we will live and the kind of people we will be, we get stronger. As we self-determine, in line with our conscience, we develop our souls while becoming more fully ourselves.

This was the progression not only for Katie and Eric, but also for Hugh and Eloise (from chapter 5). Through honest conversations and growing self-awareness, both couples shifted from relying on external approval to developing deeper internal alignment—from pursuing validation to practicing self-authorship. This shift made them stronger: more at peace within themselves and more capable of truly knowing and loving each other. As we'll see in the next two chapters, Hugh and Eloise's relationship continued to evolve, shaping not just the intimacy of their sexual relationship, but the spiritual richness of their sexual connection as well.

CHAPTER 6: SELF-REFLECTION QUESTIONS

1. Name an issue / habit / behavior of yours that
    your spouse finds difficult and (in the honesty of
    your heart) you don't fully respect either. In other
    words, name an area where your spouse doesn't
    validate you—one that, if you are honest, you
    can't fully justify either (e.g., you spend too much
    money, play mindless games on your phone, are
    unduly pessimistic to avoid disappointment, don't
    listen attentively, etc.).

2. Perhaps this issue doesn't bother you as much as
    it does your spouse, but you can admit that you
    lack integrity around it (in other words, you know
    it's not coming from the best in you). What makes
    sense about your spouse disliking this part of you?
    How does it impact them negatively? How does your
    behavior impact your feelings about yourself?

- -
- -
- -
- -
- -
- -
- -
- -
- -

3. If you were to live with more integrity—more alignment between your conscience and your behavior—what would you do differently?

4. How would addressing this issue shape how you feel about yourself? How would it change your marriage? (If you live truer to your conscience, you live truer to the marriage. This is self-authoring in action.)

SPIRITUAL DEVELOPMENT & THE INTEGRATION OF SEXUALITY

7

"Sex and spirit are linked through love, their common denominator."
—Marybeth Raynes

THE EVOLVING RELATIONSHIP BETWEEN SEXUALITY & SPIRITUALITY

As we explored in the previous chapter, the way we see ourselves—and how we relate to others—shifts as we grow through the stages of development. Naturally, this soul development touches every part of our lives. In particular, it shapes how we experience both our sexuality and our sense of the sacred. In this chapter, we'll take a closer look at these two powerful forms of relationship—our spirituality and our sexuality—and explore how they relate to each other, including how they evolve as we do. (☞ See following spread.)

Let's take a closer look at how sexuality and spirituality evolve during each developmental stage and explore how these two dimensions of our lives find progressively common ground.

STAGE 1: SEXUAL IMPULSIVITY

STAGE 2: SEXUAL INHIBITION

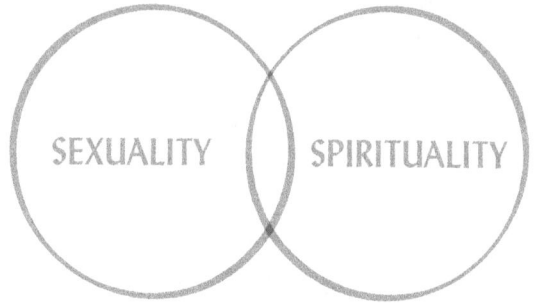

STAGE 3: SEXUAL INTEGRATION

☞ The egocentric mind (**STAGE 1**), is defined by pleasure-seeking and *impulsivity*. We understand spirituality—or *being good*—in terms of compliance with authority. Because our pleasure-seeking behavior is often out of line with the expectations of authority figures (like parents and teachers), sexuality and spirituality seem to be in direct conflict with one another. As we mature into the social stage (**STAGE 2**), we become more aware of other people and learn to *inhibit* our sexual impulses. We focus on living up to the expectations of our community, including what's seen as proper sexual behavior. We experience some overlap of sexuality and spirituality when we comply with those standards—seeing sex as good when it occurs in marriage, for example. It is not until we move into the self-authoring mind (**STAGE 3**), that we begin to truly *integrate* our sexuality. Instead of just following rules, we start to make choices that reflect our deeper values and conscience. We come into greater peace with our sexual nature, and instead of suppressing it, we begin to *inhabit* it. We are able to love and take pleasure in another soul in this stage and create moments of communion through our sexuality. It is in this stage that our sensuality and spirituality can nourish and support one another.

STAGE 1: SEXUALITY & SPIRITUALITY IN THE EGOCENTRIC MIND

When we are very young, we are naturally impulsive and preoccupied with our own needs and emotions, instinctively drawn to whatever brings us pleasure. A toddler, for example, might reach down his pants in public or strip down just before a guest arrives—simply because it feels good. Because we act on our immediate desires in this stage without considering the consequences, we rely upon authority figures to help us manage our behaviors. In other words, *self*-regulation is something we have yet to develop.

In the egocentric stage, our main concern is self-preservation—we're focused on staying safe and avoiding trouble. Because of that, our sense of right and wrong centers around pleasing authority figures, whether it's our parents or even God. We tend to follow the rules, not because we understand or agree with them, but because we want to avoid punishment or earn rewards. That dynamic can put us at odds with our natural desire to indulge, but the promise of approval or blessing often keeps us in line. At this stage, we don't yet grasp the deeper meaning behind the rules—we stick to the letter of the law. Morality feels black and white, and it's all about behavior: "Do this. Don't do that."

Part of our understood purpose on earth is to come to know God, but our understanding of God depends upon our maturity. Indeed, how far we have progressed in our development deeply shapes who we understand God to be. In the self-orientation of STAGE 1, we tend to view God in transactional terms—the one who "giveth and taketh away." Many people carry this perspective into adulthood, viewing God as one who grants blessings for obedience and withholds them for disobedience. In fact, some Latter-day Saints in this stage express their commitment to practices like temple attendance or tithing as a way to "earn blessings" or "put needed blessings in the bank."

In the STAGE 1 mind, the same God that expects compliance also rejects sensuality, treating bodily pleasure as indulgent and at odds with righteousness. Sigmund Freud captured this internal struggle in his theory of the conflict between the Super-ego (authority) and the Id (our instinct for pleasure). Because so many of us grow up linking pleasure with wrongdoing, it's not uncommon to get stuck in this early stage of sexual development. And when sex is seen as something inherently unholy, it becomes nearly impossible to build the kind of self-acceptance and integration that intimacy in marriage really requires.

This was the case for Stella, a woman who sought my help for her total lack of sexual desire. Stella had grown up in a controlling and punitive family. As a teen, her parents made it clear that they did not want her in any exclusive relationship. So, when she started dating a "nice-enough" boy at age sixteen, her parents micromanaged every interaction she had with him, even accusing her of having sex when she wasn't. Their punishments were preemptive and excessive. And their disproportionate control, combined with the cautionary messages she heard at church about the dangers of sex, led Stella to shut down her sexual feelings entirely. In her mind, the only way to avoid the adversary (in every sense) was to reject her sexuality altogether—and so she did. In fact, she buried her desires so deeply that even after marriage, they remained inaccessible. Through tears, she confessed, "I shut down my sexuality to be good. I buried it deep inside. And now, I am broken, and my marriage is broken, too."

While some people completely shut down their sexuality, like Stella did, others swing between suppressing it and giving in to it. They experience sex as dangerous and thrilling—an intoxicating rebellion against the perceived control that authority represents in the egocentric mind. But the flight into pleasure is usually short-lived, followed by consuming feelings of shame and a renewed commitment to rigid self-discipline. At this stage, sexual choices are mostly driven by fear of consequences—whether it's disappointing a spouse, upsetting a church leader, or letting down another authority figure. But when those external controls are absent, a person in the egocentric stage often finds themselves indulging once again.

It's often those who most strongly condemn sexuality who are themselves caught in a STAGE 1 struggle with their own sexual thoughts and behaviors. Their vocal objections—whether criticizing women's dress or warning against the dangers of masturbation—often function as a defense against the temptations they feel and fear might overpower their self-control.

Many individuals who consider themselves "sex addicts" are operating within this developmental stage. Unfortunately, many treatment programs are grounded in the same (STAGE 1) moral reasoning that gave rise to the unwanted behaviors in the first place. Far from providing long-term fixes for the struggles with self-regulation, these programs too often prescribe solutions that unwittingly reinforce the root problem.

As a case in point, a married man, Theo, came to me after participating in a well-known, "gospel-oriented" pornography treatment program (not affiliated with the Church) that equates attraction and arousal with sin. In this program, Theo was taught that he is engaged in a noble battle against Satan, who exerts his influence through bodily temptation. The program's initial phase, titled "Your Battle Plan: How to Beat Satan," describes the "chemical phase" of arousal as the moment when "the devil, his minions, [and] tempters enter the picture." Sexual desire is framed as a dangerous "trap" set by Satan to lead good souls astray.

The problem for Theo was that the "treatment" only intensified his preoccupation with sex. Believing that "Satan's minions" were in his body seeking to control him through his sexuality, he became more unsettled in his own skin as well as

177

hyper-vigilant around sexual feelings of any kind. When he saw an attractive woman coming down the street, for example, he regarded her more as a threat—as an agent of Satan's trap—than as a human being. By the time Theo came to me for help, he was more anxious than ever—with less sexual agency and peace with himself than he started with.

For those in this stage (including the practitioners of such a model), the sensuality of the body seems to put us in a never-ending struggle—a struggle that threatens to divide us from God. And this sense of powerlessness keeps many of us dependent upon authority figures to help us regulate our sexual choices. Even if we succeed in resisting the draw of the body (as Stella did), the fear driving that restraint usually interferes with the deeper integration of our feelings and greater agency in our choices.

Not all adults in a STAGE I mindset struggle with sexual compulsivity or repression, but their approach to sexuality remains largely self-focused. Some see sex as a fundamental "need" or "drive," expecting their spouse to fulfill that need. Some withhold sex to avoid the inconvenience of their partner's sexual desires, while others still engage in sex primarily to prevent conflict or to avoid negative personal consequences. In each case, the interaction is shaped by self-interest rather than love or desire for another.

Understandably, ego-driven sex precludes intimacy or love. In a moment of growing self-awareness, my client Cole acknowledged, "When Clara finally agrees to sex, I get so lost in the rush of pleasure that I completely lose track of her—like I'm in a trance." Clara's sense of being used during sex wasn't imagined—she was, in fact, a means to his end. Sex was about his gratification, which understandably made sex entirely undesirable for her.

Those of us who grew up in very controlling or chaotic environments (as Stella did), may struggle to move beyond the egocentric stage of sexual development. Without the stability and security needed for healthy self-regulation, it can be challenging to relate to sex in a way that enriches our lives. When we've experienced sexual harm—such as abuse or violation—it's completely understandable to reject sex altogether. In doing so, we're often trying to restore a sense of safety, which is a core priority of the **STAGE I** mind. It is also not uncommon for many well-intentioned church members to instinctively teach messages about the destructiveness of sex or the incompatibility of sex with goodness—because this has been their lived experience.

Some adults perpetually stuck in this stage may exhibit traits of antisocial or narcissistic personality disorders, which hinder compassion and self-awareness and allow them to objectify and sexually exploit others.

STAGE 2: SEXUALITY & SPIRITUALITY IN THE SOCIAL MIND

When we enter the second stage of development, we no longer focus simply on how our choices affect us alone. The need to belong becomes paramount in the social stage and motivates us to understand and align with the expectations of those around us. We become more attuned to how our choices affect others and, in our desire for acceptance, we tend to absorb and follow the values of our group—including its views on sex.

As members of the Church, this means we strive to live by the law of chastity. The expectations of sexual abstinence before marriage and fidelity within it teaches us the value of managing our sexual impulses. Self-restraint—an important developmental goal of STAGE 2—is important to our eventual sexual integration and agency. Just as a car needs functional brakes to reach its destination safely, we must learn to manage our impulses to function in life well—sexual impulses included. At the very least, sexual self-control is essential for honoring commitments and maintaining fidelity.

Our desire for social acceptance plays an important role in learning to manage our impulses. We don't want to lose the approval of our community or God—especially in matters as consequential as sex. So, we are highly motivated to develop the self-control necessary to follow Church teachings.

While this is an important motivation, our desire for acceptance can also be misused. For instance, sexual purity object lessons or the framing of *worthiness* interviews can be used to imply that sexual behavior diminishes our value. Beyond being theologically flawed, this perspective can cultivate shame, making it harder for us to accept ourselves and integrate our sexuality. As teachers and leaders, we must be intentional in how we convey these values, so that we do not unintentionally interfere with our children's comprehension of God's love for them or hinder their ability to make wise decisions around sex. (See chapter 10 for more on fostering healthy sexual integration in children.)

Our moral reasoning in the social stage is still largely behavioral and concrete, with moral authority still rooted outside of ourselves. This means we often fixate on whether specific sexual behaviors are "right" or "wrong." It's common for clients to ask me—as someone they see as an authority—whether certain sexual acts are morally acceptable. "Is it okay to touch yourself as long as your spouse is present?" "Is sexual fantasy okay?" They want to know what I think, and they want to know how other Latter-day Saints think. They are leveraging the mind of the group to interpret and navigate their own beliefs and decisions.

In the social stage, we understand that sex *can* be good in the right setting. Church leaders reassure us that "the intimate relationship between husbands and wives is good and honorable in the eyes of God."[1] Sex in marriage is considered worthy and not inherently in conflict with our spirituality. Yet even here, the connection between sexuality and spirituality remains thin, as we continue to hold mixed beliefs about whether sex is something sacred or suspect. In the same talk teaching us that sex in marriage is good, for example, we are also cautioned against "unnatural" sexual behaviors: "Keep yourselves above any domineering or unworthy behavior in the tender, intimate relationship between husband and wife." The suggestion that sexual behavior can easily become "unworthy" (albeit in this ill-defined way) can introduce an undercurrent of anxiety within a marital relationship.

Of course, being considerate in a sexual relationship is always important. But if we imagine that eroticism is risky or barely acceptable to God, we will bring an unhelpful vigilance and self-consciousness to the marriage bed that interferes with authenticity and ease. As a workshop participant confided, "I like sex, but I feel so uncomfortable knowing that God is watching us." Similarly, a friend once joked, "It's hard to relax when 'angels above us are silent notes taking!'"[2]

With too little confidence that God views sexuality as a valuable part of our humanity, many of us in the social mind limit sexual frequency or gravitate to sexual routines that are emotionally and erotically guarded. Since we are still managing how much of our (sexual) selves we reveal, sexuality and spirituality rarely intersect in **STAGE 2**. In other words, while sex can bring both pleasure and connection in the social mind, our limited tolerance of intimacy and sexual openness prevents it from reaching the deeper layers of the soul.

Think back to Hugh and Eloise's story from chapter 5 and how they related to sex before crossing the "continental divide": Eloise had learned to see sex as a lesser part of herself, so she was hesitant to really embrace it. She was also quite sensitive to what others expected of her and how they might judge her, so the idea of being truly known—especially in sex—was unnerving. Eloise had convinced herself that denying pleasure was more righteous than enjoying it. She took refuge in the emotional distance of accommodating Hugh once a week. Though she cared about Hugh, she had no desire to know him beyond what made her feel secure and what made her feel good about herself. This meant she dismissed any of Hugh's desires that unsettled her, even though it meant leaving much of him unknown to her.

Hugh, for his part, professed to want intimacy, but his actions told a different story. Because of *his* dependence on social approval, he avoided exposing conversations with Eloise—especially about the parts of himself he wasn't proud of. Rather than risk her rejection, he kept many things to himself, while quietly resenting Eloise's limited interest in him.

The truth was that Hugh's desire wasn't so much for his wife as it was for her sexual acceptance—something he depended upon too much to feel okay. Like Eloise, he wasn't yet capable of fully knowing his spouse, let alone desiring her as a whole person. He, too, was still trying to sort out his own worthiness, and that struggle made it difficult for him to be truly known sexually—or to fully know his wife.

When we are operating from the social mind and don't get the validation we want from a spouse, it's natural to either pull away or push them to act in ways that make us feel better about ourselves. That's exactly what Hugh and Eloise were doing, even though neither of them understood their behavior as needy. Instead, as most of us do, they each told themselves stories that justified their behavior and helped them feel in control, while reinforcing their emotional dependence on each other. This dynamic held until intimacy—*becoming more known to each other*—began to unravel the collusive alliance they'd been living.

As Hugh and Eloise started to see themselves through each other's eyes, they could no longer avoid the hard truths that were becoming clear. What they saw pushed them to face the painful reality that they were hurting the person they loved. That realization didn't just bring guilt—it sparked a sincere desire to grow and love each other better. By choosing to be honest with themselves and to do better, each of them crossed that important threshold of growth into **STAGE 3**—becoming more grounded in their truest selves.

Love asks us to be honest and face what is true. It never asks us to surrender to another person, but to surrender to what is right and what is real. That's what Hugh and Eloise did, and they did not lose themselves in the process. Instead, they let go of their lesser selves—their egos and self-service—for something stronger and more trustworthy. And as a result, they became more able to love, more capable of intimacy, and more fully *a couple*.

STAGE 3: SEXUALITY & SPIRITUALITY IN THE SELF-AUTHORING MIND

"Love is not a matter of finding the right person, but of seeing the person you love as they are."
— *Rainer Maria Rilke*

Through the stories of Hugh and Eloise, and of Katie and Eric, we see the shift toward greater psychological autonomy and integrity that defines the self-authoring stage. **STAGE 3** is marked by a deepening ability to be true to ourselves at the same time that we're able to love and value another person. Philosopher Martin Buber describes this transformation as movement from "I-It" relationships—where others are seen as objects or tools for our own purposes—to "I-Thou" relationships, where we honor the full humanity of the other.

This evolution in how we love shapes both the meaning of sex and its connection to our spirituality. In a **STAGE 1** mind, we want sex for the physical pleasure it brings. In **STAGE 2**, we want sex for the validation it offers us. But in **STAGE 3**, sex becomes a way of knowing—a way of witnessing and cherishing another soul. Sex in this stage is a way of taking deep pleasure in another's existence. This kind of embodied communion opens us up to the spiritual beauty in the world and each other. And these moments of deep connection strengthen our souls and our faith.

Stage 3: Sexuality & Spirituality in the Self-authoring Mind

TO KNOW YOU IS TO LOVE YOU

Because we no longer relate to others as an extension of ourselves in this stage, we are freer to truly know a spouse—their history, their desires, their experiences and sorrows. We are able to know even the parts of them that challenge and unsettle us. Similarly, we can desire another for who they are. **STAGE 3** desire is not about possession or gratification. It's not about filling a void or getting something for ourselves. Rather, to desire another soul is to cherish them and to love them. It expresses itself not just in the desire to be with them, but also in our willingness to make sacrifices on their behalf. It is to invest ourselves in our spouse's wellbeing.

Perhaps paradoxically, it's our ability to value our spouse's individuality—the very ways they are *not* like us—that deepens attraction in long-term love. We no longer need or want a partner who simply reinforces us or reflects us back to ourselves. Instead, we desire that they are fully themselves. It is precisely the mystery and challenge of their differences that fuels our longing in marriage—the longing to engage, again and again, with the parts of them we don't yet fully know. This is how we continue to desire what is already ours—how we long for the very person right in front of us.

The more we are able to love a spouse as they are, the more deeply we can also accept ourselves. As our capacity to embrace our shared humanity deepens, the nature and meaning of our eroticism also matures. No longer driven by anxiety or compulsivity, we can approach our sexual desires with greater curiosity, acceptance, and even humor. We no longer regard our (sometimes unruly) sexual thoughts as threats; instead, we see them as opportunities to better understand ourselves and a spouse. And out of our deepening self-awareness, we are able to make intentional choices—ones that respect both partners and nurture a stronger, more intimate marriage.

FAITH & INTIMATE SURRENDER

As we integrate our sexuality and trust ourselves more deeply, we can bring an openness to sex that makes room for something soulful, even transcendent. In intimate moments of meeting, we can experience a deep reassurance—a kind of renewal—in being truly known and enjoyed, body and soul. In this way, lovemaking takes on a sacred quality in marriage. It becomes a form of communion and care—something that can steady and strengthen the soul of the marriage. While we cannot force these transcendent moments, when they arise, they are a kind of grace.

Cultivating this kind of soulful intimacy takes more than attraction—it requires our faith. Not only faith in our partner, but faith in ourselves: in the truth of our own worthiness and the truth of theirs. Because to let another soul touch us, to allow divine love to move through us, we must be willing to lower our guard—to risk being truly seen. That kind of surrender is not weakness; it is strength. It is a deliberate letting go of ego and control in the hope that we are worthy of love and capable of loving in return.

To see how this unfolds in practice, let's return to the story of Hugh and Eloise. By sacrificing their pursuit of validation and courageously taking deeper responsibility for themselves, they grew into a more collaborative relationship. In showing up honestly and bringing their full selves to one another, they laid the foundation for a rich, open-hearted sexual relationship. In the next chapter, we'll discover how they grew into a couple who could experience deep pleasure together—pleasure that nourished not only their relationship, but their souls and their faith.

DISCOVERING THE SOUL OF SEX

8

"If you're like most people, you don't just want sex to satisfy you. You want sex to inspire you. ...It's crucial when you go looking for erotic inspiration, that you look first within yourself."
—Stephen Snyder, M.D.

THE ELUSIVENESS OF DESIRE

Eloise was quite reserved when we first started meeting together—cautious of the vulnerability and accountability that any good therapy calls for. But once she had made the conscious decision to fully invest in her marriage and sexual relationship, she began speaking more openly about her experience of sex with Hugh. She wasn't bringing up issues to justify herself, she was courageously exposing her mind—being more *intimate*—out of her desire to make their sexual relationship better. Her courageous honesty was a testament to her deepening commitment to their marriage.

During one meeting, Eloise confessed that while she was enjoying their sexual interactions more than ever, she longed for more physical desire—like she used to feel. "I genuinely look forward to being with Hugh. I can even feel excited for him to come home. But then, once we are together—my arousal just evaporates. And I don't know why!" Eloise explained. "I hate that I'm probably going to disappoint him all over again. I feel like something is wrong with me—"

"You mean when you don't orgasm?" Hugh asked.

"Well, yeah—and because I don't have the desire and passion you wish I did—and that *I* wish I did. I want to be excited—not just *willing*. So, when I can't get there, it's so frustrating. I know you're trying so hard to help me, but I feel bad that arousal and orgasm take such a long time, if they happen at all."

"I don't mind if it takes a while," Hugh said. "I just want you to have pleasure."

"I'm not going to bail on sex," Eloise said, "but it feels like more work than it's worth sometimes! When I avoid sex, it's not because I don't love you or think you are attractive. I just wish sex were an easier place for me, I guess."

Throughout their marriage, Hugh had made a sincere effort to be a good lover, attentively asking about Eloise's likes and dislikes, and doing whatever he could to pleasure her. The challenge, however, was that Eloise usually didn't know what would excite her. Though well-intentioned, his questions usually created more pressure than passion, leaving Eloise uncertain and Hugh increasingly powerless.

What we often don't realize is that feeling good about ourselves is one of the most powerful aphrodisiacs. We are most drawn to sex when it affirms our sense of worth. At its best, sex is a deep affirmation of who we are; it is to be accepted and *enjoyed* exactly as we are. This freedom to be fully ourselves is essential to keeping eros alive in long-term, intimate love.

Hugh and Eloise were each seeking reassurance and approval in their intimate encounters, yet they each felt measured and inadequate. Few things dampen desire more than the weight of perceived judgment. The moment sex becomes a means of proving something—our worth, our desirability, or our love for a partner—its life-giving energy is suffocated. As soon as we give sex a job to do, it rebels.

Because in recent weeks Eloise had consciously reaffirmed her commitment to her marriage, this act of self-determination had strengthened her sense of autonomy in the relationship. Eloise's sense of obligation that once weighed their marriage down had lifted. Yet, in their sexual relationship—where they both felt less secure—Eloise often found herself reverting to an instinctive need for approval, hoping her body and sexuality would serve as proof of her love for Hugh and her worthiness as a lover.

Hugh was also trying to prove himself in sex. He regarded his wife's limited arousal and pleasure as evidence of his limited desirability and sexual prowess. He hoped if he *served her needs*—putting her pleasure above his own—this would make him and his sexuality more worthy. So, Eloise's sexual interest and pleasure became a measure of him. Naturally, the pressure to elicit a response that neither of them could fully control only heightened their anxiety and diminished their mutual enjoyment.

"You are both working too hard," I said.

"Working too hard? What do you mean?" Hugh asked.

"If you want your intimate relationship to be a place of connection and joy, you need to stop asking it to prove so much. You're burdening sex in a way that kills arousal—taking too much responsibility for the other's experience, when it's not your job and not in your control."

"But isn't it *good* that I care about Eloise? I really want to give her a positive experience."

"Well, caring about Eloise and *trying to give her pleasure* are not necessarily the same thing," I said. "I'm sure she can sense that you're working hard for her orgasm, and she doesn't want to let you down."

"I know you don't want me to feel pressured, but I do," Eloise admitted, "When you spend so much time on me, I feel the pressure to not disappoint, and then it seems I almost certainly will."

Humans are very good at mapping meaning in sex. Eloise was mapping Hugh's mind, whether or not he wanted her to. She was tracking Hugh's motivations and anxieties and trying to manage them through her body's pleasure, which made it almost certain that her passion and sexual responsiveness would be minimal.

"But why is that a problem?" Hugh asked, "What's wrong with wanting to pleasure Eloise?"

"If Eloise tracks that you need her to experience orgasm for you to feel okay about her—or to feel okay about you—then she's isn't free. In needing to manage both of your egos, the sexual experience cannot be unselfconscious and joyful. In other words, she's absorbing your anxiety, which only adds to hers."

"*My* anxiety?—I don't think I'm anxious," Hugh said, with a hint of defensiveness.

"Well, whenever you're trying to prove something about yourself through sex—especially something beyond your control, such as how much pleasure Eloise feels—you're going to experience anxiety. It's that sense of powerlessness or futility that comes from trying to make happen something that you cannot make happen. You cannot get your wife to feel what you want her to feel."

Hugh considered my words.

"Even if the two of you *succeed*—as in climax," I continued, "you're both too self-conscious to truly let go or experience the kind of psychological surrender that makes sex so wonderful."

There are, of course, many generous men who engage with their wives in ways that enhance the pleasure of both. But for Hugh, his attention wasn't simply an unselfconscious gift. He wanted Eloise to enjoy sex so she would want it more. He also wanted to feel like a good lover. In this way, his attentiveness carried ego needs that subtly shaped their experience. Hugh's quiet pressure—and Eloise's attempts not to disappoint—created a knot of sexual anxiety between them, one that tightened each time either felt the need to perform or prove something in sex. What they needed was a way to move beyond their self-consciousness to find a deeper soul connection through their bodies.

Psychologist Murray Bowen observed that anxiety is highly contagious in couples, even if this transmission is difficult to track. This is especially true in sex. We cannot help but map the intentions and feelings of a partner in intimate contact. The ability to read each other's inner world is part of what makes sex such a powerful way to share our souls. But this is also why we can struggle to hold onto who we are and what we're responsible for in our intimate relationships. Even those of us who feel relatively grounded in our day-to-day lives may struggle when mapping an entitled, needy, or disengaged partner.

"I understand what you're saying. It makes sense to me that tracking Hugh's desires makes me feel pressure and that is unhelpful. But how do I get myself to feel more passion, then?" Eloise asked. "I really want to feel desire."

"The problem is you can't *make* yourself desire. In fact, the harder you try to summon it, the more elusive it will be. Much like falling asleep, desire is something you surrender to rather than force. And the very best sex is never hard work. Good sex is easy."

"So, then, what can we do about that?" Hugh asked.

"I would suggest that rather than chase a specific outcome, you each focus on accepting yourselves and each other just as you are. Let your only goal be to settle down together in any intimate moment."

Dr. David Schnarch, who expanded on Bowen's theory of psychological enmeshment, introduced the practice of "hugging until relaxed"—an exercise designed to help individuals *self*-regulate in intimate contact. Couples stand firmly on their own feet, wrap their arms around each other, and focus on settling down as deeply as they can (ideally for 8 to 10 minutes). As couples calm their bodies, they are more able to move from an anxious psychological fusion with their partner's mind to the psychological autonomy of **STAGE 3**. In other words, hugging until relaxed uses the body to help individuals *self*-soothe into deeper differentiation, even while tracking the desires, judgments, and dysregulations of their spouse.

As a Buddhist saying goes, only when the mind is calm can we know things as they actually are. ☞ When we quiet our minds in intimate contact, we are more able to know a spouse without losing our ability to belong to ourselves. We can stay anchored in who we are, even while knowing the differences and pressures that are a part of the relationship. As couples grow more secure in themselves while staying deeply connected to their spouse, they develop the ease that forms the emotional foundation of intimate sex.

☞ For instance, Ajahn Chah, a Thai forest monk, taught: "When the mind is still, it reflects reality clearly; but when it is clouded by desire and aversion, it distorts what is true. Calm the mind, and you will see things as they are."

For Eloise and Hugh, the ability to self-author—to reference their own desires and beliefs—was a capacity they were getting better at in their emotional relationship, but it was not yet a reliable part of their physical relationship. In the high-meaning context of sex, they regressed back to the performative self of STAGE 2. Learning to stay true to themselves in an embodied way was especially important for an *intimate* sexual relationship.

"Being calm in your own mind and body is important to eros," I explained. "This ease is critical to your sense of authenticity and freedom in sex. It's a little paradoxical that the more you connect to your inner ease, the closer you can be to your spouse—emotionally and physically. By contrast, the more you try to 'feel connected' or 'feel desire,' the more anxious and out of sync you will be.

"So, are you saying that calming myself down while with Hugh will get me aroused?" Eloise asked, a bit skeptically.

"Well, certainly there is no guarantee," I replied. "But for many of us, the calm of self-acceptance creates the space in which desire can take root. And if it doesn't, that's okay, too. You simply have another opportunity to quiet your mind, accept yourself, and be in the stillness together. This mutual acceptance is absolutely the foundation of any sustainable erotic relationship. So, for now, that's your only goal."

A suggestion from sex therapist Stephen Snyder is similar to Schnarch's "Hugging until relaxed" exercise. He recommends that couples go to bed with no agenda except to lie naked together. The goal is simply to be present with one another in the mutual exposure. Paying attention to bodily sensations—such as the softness of the sheets against one's skin or the natural rhythm of one's breath—can facilitate a state of ease. Dr. Snyder suggests that this first step of lying naked together can include conversation or relaxing touch, but the primary objective is finding an inner calm in the sensuality and proximity. Far more than intercourse or orgasm, acceptance and shared moments of peace are the lifeblood of a sexual relationship—and the source of a sustainable eroticism in a long-term sexual relationship.

"What if I start to feel aroused?" Eloise asked.

"For now, if you feel aroused, just enjoy it, but hold off on doing anything explicitly sexual," I explained. "It is important that your reflexive urge to chase an outcome doesn't take over."

When Hugh and Eloise tried this approach the results were promising. When they returned a week later, they reported that their time together, free of demands, had felt really good. "Our nightly ritual of going to bed naked was surprisingly more enjoyable than most of our sexual experiences," Hugh reflected. "Since we were purposefully avoiding sex, I didn't expect to feel so connected to Eloise." Hugh told me that initially he felt the impulse to either repress his sexual feelings or to start touching Eloise.

"It was strange to just experience the arousal and take it in. I felt aroused most nights we got in bed. It was hard not to—given the sensuality of it all and the imposed limits we created. But I did as you said, and just tried to calm myself and enjoy the sexual feelings—which I got better at."

Eloise reported feeling quite hesitant at first. She feared that getting in bed naked and doing nothing would either obligate her or prove her deficient in some way. What if relaxing turned out to be the only thing she wanted to do with Hugh? What if she began to feel desire and then was more obligated by this supposed cure? Despite her fears and anxieties, Eloise courageously chose to show up anyway—driven by her commitment to herself and her desire to build an intimate marriage.

Lying naked in the stillness, Eloise noticed how very anxious she was—how unaccustomed she was to just *being* with Hugh while not producing, distracting, or running from the interaction. These were all impulses she knew well, but as she calmed her heart, she could also see that Hugh was okay. And in her growing calm, she began to feel a lot of gratitude for him—for his friendship and his growing investment in their marriage. When she let go of having anything to prove, she found herself drawn to him—captivated by the definition of his jawline and the gentle curls in his hair.

These feelings of attraction made her a little anxious, but it helped to remind herself that neither Hugh's arousal nor hers required anything of her—that she could simply *be* for now. In her growing stillness, Eloise was discovering a deeper ability to be present with herself. And in turn, a deeper ability to be present with Hugh.

ENJOYMENT WITHOUT EXPECTATION

Hugh and Eloise were ready to step toward more sexual engagement, but it was crucial that they not take the arousal they were feeling and regress into a goal-oriented mindset. So, as Snyder recommends, I suggested that they try to hold onto the ease and openness they were feeling while deliberately turning their attention to each other.

"Avoid trying to arouse each other," I advised. "Instead, focus on *experiencing* one another—notice the scent of their neck, the feel of their lips, or the curve of their waist. You don't need to feel desire to begin; you only need to be open to going where the experience leads you. If arousal comes, then let it nourish you, but don't chase it or force it. And certainly, don't pressure yourself to reach orgasm," I added. "In fact, if anything starts to feel like a lot of work, stop doing it."

"Stop doing it?" Hugh asked a little confused.

"Yes, if sex starts to feel like effort, pause and go back to whatever was bringing you enjoyment before. You can certainly do things that encourage your arousal if you want to, but make sure you don't start working too hard to get anywhere. Sexuality thrives on freedom, so if you proceed when it feels like a struggle, your natural desire for physical connection will likely decrease."

Knowing that both Hugh and Eloise tended to get preoccupied with what would "satisfy" or give pleasure to the other, I recommended that they focus on *taking* pleasure instead. This was an especially important shift for Eloise who instinctively related to sex in the libido-killing form of a dutiful accommodation. To move into the energy of eros, I suggested that she, in particular, think entirely in terms of *taking* pleasure for herself in Hugh's body.

"I like that idea, but it's a little weird for me. Shouldn't I be doing what makes Hugh feel loved?" Eloise asked.

"Definitely not—especially because taking care of his needs or 'making him feel loved' feels burdensome for you," I said. "In really good lovemaking, we are primarily taking pleasure in our partner's body and existence—not taking care of them. This is what we do with our own babies: we caress and kiss them—we eat them up, because their sweet, little sensual selves give us so much joy. We are not considering *what feels good to the baby*. We are simply taking pleasure in them. And it's as good for the baby as it is for the parent. It communicates that the child's existence is good, that their presence fills us with joy."

"Unsurprisingly, that's the same validating energy we want in sex—we want to enjoy and be fully enjoyed again, exactly as we are. Just like C.S. Lewis observed, when we are in the energy of eros, the distinction between giving and receiving gets obliterated," I explained.[1]

Feeling the freedom in this suggestion, Eloise admitted that taking pleasure in Hugh felt intuitively more desirable than trying to fulfill his assumed needs in sex. Hugh, too, liked the idea of being enjoyed, although this perspective challenged what he had been taught about how to relate to a woman. Hugh had internalized the message that sex was made legitimate if it was an act of service to a spouse. He also believed protecting women was a core virtue of a good man, making him very wary of being an imposition. (In fact, this fear had made the impersonal nature of pornography feel like a safer way to be sexual.) As a result, he instinctively focused on Eloise's pleasure as a way to justify his own—if she didn't enjoy it, did he even have a right to his own pleasure?

Hugh's cautiousness and Eloise's pressure on herself to be "selfless" were both rooted in a desire to fulfill inherited roles and feel legitimate in their sexuality. Yet these efforts often stood in the way of a deeper openness and authenticity with each other. Afraid of being an imposition, Hugh held back from initiating or flirting, usually waiting for Eloise to show interest before revealing his own. Meanwhile, Eloise was slow to flirt or dress in a way that might spark desire, because she didn't want to be obligated if her behavior turned Hugh on. Still, she longed for the reassurance of being desired. But without much sexual energy coming from Hugh, it became progressively harder to access her own.

Most women's sexual interest is deeply tied to feeling desired and pursued, even in marriage. Women simply have more on the line when they are sexual, including the risks of disease, pregnancy, and unrequited emotional attachment. So, women are naturally pickier about whom they let into their lives and bodies. Since male sexuality is often perceived as less discriminating or committed, a man's persistent pursuit of a particular woman (and not simply of sex itself) can awaken her interest. When a woman sees a man invested enough to pursue her despite her reluctance, she is more likely to desire him in return. Given this psychobiology, the turn-on for most women is *being the turn-on*. Most women don't want to give pleasure as much as they want the deep pleasure of surrendering to a lover's desire.

Because of this common sexual dynamic in heterosexual relationships, coupled with Hugh's history with pornography, Eloise sometimes questioned whether his desire was truly for *her* or just for sex in general. To address this, I encouraged Hugh to initiate moments of "simmering" with Eloise—intentionally savoring sexual feelings with her throughout the day, but without any pressure or expectation of it leading to more.

"Whenever you feel attracted to Eloise," I said, "express it to her—let her feel your attraction in the way you touch her. Lean into her and savor a moment of sensual connection. In other words,

202

show her your longing for her, but let her also see your self-control. By enjoying her without expectation of any sexual engagement later, you'll help her know she is free and genuinely desired—two key elements that cultivate a woman's sexual interest. And Eloise, your role is simply to receive his attention—to open your heart and allow yourself to enjoy it."

The value of non-demand arousal in marriage is central to Tantric practice, an Eastern tradition that emphasizes the spiritual value of eros. In a state of arousal, our perception of time slows and our awareness of beauty and wonder deepens. This heightened awareness allows us to see mystery and depth in a partner in ways that a rushed or anxious mind cannot perceive. Tantric philosophy views harnessing this state of mind as not only important to intimacy and joy in sex but also to our spiritual perception—making it easier to witness the transcendent nature of love in an erotically elevated state.

Tantric practice, just like simmering, is to engage in activities that build arousal while intentionally delaying orgasm over a prolonged period. This might include enjoying erotic touch over multiple days before permitting oneself to move to climax. In the deliberate embrace of erotic energy, couples increase their capacity for desire and pleasure together as well as deepen their connection.

This recommended shift in focus brought remarkable results. In the weeks following our conversation, Hugh and Eloise experienced the deepest pleasure and most uninhibited desire of their marriage. Hugh took multiple opportunities to simmer Eloise—lingering in a kiss before leaving for work, gazing at her with obvious admiration from across the room, and savoring arousal with her as they lay in bed at night before drifting off to sleep.

As Hugh was learning to enjoy Eloise erotically without any pressure to move to intercourse or orgasm, Eloise felt progressively freer to receive his sexual energy. In fact, she realized how much she had missed his sexual attention. Hugh's erotic interest and Eloise's receptivity began to resemble the passion of their early days and reignited a sense of excitement that they each had missed.

What surprised them both is that they could *feel* the energetic difference in each other's touch. In the past, Hugh's touch could fill Eloise with a sense of burden because it revealed his anxiety and expectation. But now, her body was mapping his attraction and pleasure in being close to her. Their touch and movement conveyed a liberating shift in meaning and Eloise's body responded with greater enthusiasm and desire for Hugh.

After several days of simmering, Hugh and Eloise's normal self-inhibition gave way to an erotic intensity. As their pent-up desire peaked, they surrendered to the raw pull between them—moaning, grasping, consumed by their hunger for each other. Afterward, Eloise and Hugh drifted off to sleep, filled with feelings of deep contentment.

By morning, however, doubt began to creep in. Their experience the night before had been authentic, intimate, and entirely free of pressure or hesitation. And yet, the sheer intensity of their passion was unsettling for Eloise. It didn't align with the image she held of what a faithful couple's intimate lives should look like. More spiritual people wouldn't surrender to such unrestrained, embodied hunger, she thought. Although the experience had been joyful, it was also primal. They had surrendered to the body, and while it felt undeniably wonderful, she couldn't shake the lingering question: Had they done something wrong?

"Do you feel weird about last night?" Eloise asked tentatively as she was preparing breakfast.

"No—not at all," Hugh stated sincerely. "It was incredible." But the uncertainty in Eloise's voice caught his attention. Did she feel bad about their experience? Did she believe his desire had compromised her in some way? Would she be reluctant to share this kind of passion with him again?

Eloise had always been more tentative about sex than Hugh, so he was accustomed to focusing on her anxieties rather than his own. But Eloise's question triggered a spiral of self-doubt. Hugh's history with porn had conditioned him to see his sexuality as a negative force, while growing up with a mother prone to depression had instilled a deep fear of harming a woman. The convergence of these two formative experiences left Hugh convinced that harm would be the inevitable result of his uninhibited desire. Paralyzed by that assumption, he didn't ask Eloise a single follow-up question—too afraid to hear her view of their passionate evening. Instead, he stopped simmering and enjoying Eloise, and they bickered about unrelated topics instead.

When Hugh and Eloise arrived at their next appointment a few days later, they were eager to get my perspective. They each expressed a sense of happiness about the pleasure and freedom in their recent experience while emphasizing that they didn't want their pursuit of a richer sexual relationship to come at the expense of their spirituality.

"Can you tell me more about what you were afraid of?" I asked Hugh when he explained his panic the morning after their passionate encounter.

"I guess I was afraid that by letting go, my sexuality had become something harmful. Eloise was completely into it in the moment, but the raw intensity of the experience and her uncertainty the next day made me feel like I should have protected her from my desire, and maybe even from *her* desire. I wondered if I'd crossed a line somehow."

"I mean, I honestly loved feeling that kind of passion," Eloise clarified. "And we didn't cross any of our agreed upon boundaries. So, I didn't wake up with a specific concern, I just felt a vague unease . . . like, *is this the kind of thing that religious people do?* When I think of upright people, I imagine people more *in control* than that."

Hugh and Eloise were each grappling with deeply rooted beliefs about the supposed incompatibility of eroticism and spirituality—trying to reconcile their personal experiences with the values and assumptions they'd inherited. Beneath it all, they were confronting the larger question of what they believed and what kind of couple they desired to be—an essential step in their shift from a socially defined mind to a more self-determined one.

The morality of erotic love can be challenging, though. So much of our social conditioning focuses on tempering our impulses, making it easy to associate the body's sensuality with indulgence or impropriety. Even when we consciously reject the idea that sexuality is inherently sinful, our spiritual ideals of self-control and temperance make it easy to view bodily pleasure with suspicion—as if embracing it were a regression of sorts.

On top of that, the thoughts and desires that stir arousal can be bewildering in their own right, often at odds with the composed, responsible way we conduct our everyday lives. It's not always clear how to make sense of our erotic imagination. What should we make of Proverbs 23:7, "*As a man thinketh in his heart, so is he*"? It's a damning idea, indeed, if taken literally and applied to sexual thought.

But as C.S. Lewis reminds us in his book *The Four Loves*,[2] taking ourselves too seriously in sex does violence to our humanity. Often in our attempt to sanitize sex, we impose a gravity on the subject that borders on idolatry. Lewis suggests that this kind of misplaced reverence distorts our understanding of our sexual nature and undermines a needed vitality in a couple's intimate connection. "We must not attempt to find an absolute in the flesh. Banish play and laughter from the bed of love and you may let in a false goddess," he writes. "Sensible lovers laugh," he insists, suggesting that it is through delight, not solemnity, that we touch the divinity in erotic love.

In other words, our eroticism is a kind of grown-up play, a joyful retreat from our sensible lives. And as much as sexual play might seem like a departure from what is spiritual and good, Christ taught us in Matthew 7 that we can know the true nature of something by what it produces. If something we choose is good, it will bear good fruit. Alma offers the same guidance: If a seed is good, it will enlighten us and bring us joy. So, we can ask ourselves: Do our sexual choices bring us closer together or do they alienate us from ourselves or our spouse? Does the way we relate to our sexuality create deeper peace with ourselves and our marriage or does it create fracture and distrust?

"Even though you've felt frustrated in the past by Eloise's reluctance around sex, it seems you've still been operating in the belief that your sexuality is something she needs protection from," I said to Hugh. "Perhaps the real work for you is to honestly ask yourself whether there's anything truly harmful in your desire for your wife, or if what you're wrestling with is the challenge of accepting your sexual nature."

"Of course, if any of your sexual choices take advantage of Eloise, then that's something you must address," I continued. "But that's not what Eloise is claiming she experienced with you. From where I sit, this looks less like a moral failure and more like something you're being called to grow beyond. This is a chance to move past the fear you've been conditioned to feel about the sexuality God gave you," I said. "The question to ask yourself is this: Does your sensual longing for one another truly diminish you? Or might it be part of what makes you whole?"

Although Hugh and Eloise had felt some anxiety about the intensity of their desire, their sexual relationship was not a simple pursuit of gratification or use of one another. Their desire didn't express a wish to escape life, but a way to meet each other in it. It reflected their longing for each other—their embodied yearning for one another's soul. And while erotic desire is *carnal*—which is to say, "of the body"—it's an expression of love that elevates and restores us in marriage. In fact, *true* eroticism—the longing for intimate communion—is a yearning that lies at the heart of spirituality and a joyful marriage.

Eloise spoke, her voice thoughtful. "I think it has really just been fear that's held me back," she said. "The truth is, Hugh's desire for me recently has felt very good. At times it was daunting to take it in, but allowing myself to witness his pleasure in being with me was a deep pleasure for me. Maybe the doubt I've wrestled with most is whether I'm worthy of this kind of love, and perhaps related, if God is truly okay with this kind of sexual joy." Eloise paused for a moment, then added, "It feels like a better world to have faith in a God who is."

Intimate sex in marriage is indeed a kind of sacred surrender—an act of faith, even. To open our hearts to the compassion and care of a spouse requires courage. It asks us to believe not only in the reality of love itself but in our lovability. It also requires faith in a God that wants us to experience the safety and solace of intimate connection—a God who wants us to know joy through one another.

In accepting the gift of our eroticism, we become more able to love through it—and to create beauty with it. Loving sexuality has the power not only to nourish the soul, but to connect us to what is sacred—not by escaping the body but by "infusing the body and its desires with soul."[3]

Hugh turned to Eloise, full of quiet admiration and moved by the courage of the woman beside him. In intimate moments he had looked at her with a sense of awe, struck by her beauty and the wonder of being loved by her. Looking at her now, that same sense of amazement washed over him. Eloise met his gaze with a smile, receiving his pleasure in her and returning it with her own. They were a couple coming to understand that intimate love lies at the heart of spiritual wholeness—and that their sexuality was a sacred gift—a gift capable of filling their marriage with both depth and delight, humanity and joy.

CHAPTER 8: SELF-REFLECTION QUESTIONS

Whether or not we realize it, we communicate meanings
in the sex we are having (or avoiding). Our touch
communicates our desires and the meanings between us.
These meanings impact our body's responsiveness.

1. Think about the moments in your sexual relationship
    when you have felt the most freedom and ease.
    What meanings between you contributed to those
    feelings? Conversely, when have you felt restricted or
    inhibited erotically? What meanings contributed to
    your experience of inhibition?

2. How does your level of self-acceptance impact
    your experience of sexual intimacy? Can you
    recall times when feeling good about yourself
    enhanced your pleasure or connection, or when
    self-doubt hindered it?

3. This chapter discusses how having an agenda
   in sex can diminish our sense of freedom, and
   therefore can diminish desire and pleasure. Are
   there instances where your pursuit of a particular
   outcome (like orgasm or arousal) interfered with
   connection or pleasure? How might you and your
   spouse create an environment where you each feel
   freer from pressure or expectation to enjoy each
   other more completely?

4. Reflecting on your intimate interactions, what
   messages do you communicate through the way
   you touch, respond to, or avoid your spouse? What
   messages does your spouse communicate to you
   nonverbally? How do these messages relate to your
   feeling of acceptance? How do they relate to your
   feelings of desire?

----

5. Have you ever had an intimate experience that filled you with joy? Think of one such moment if you have one. What factors contributed to that sense of joy? How did you feel about your spouse? About yourself? What impact did the sexual experience have on you? What impact did it have on your relationship?

_____
_____
_____
_____
_____
_____
_____
_____
_____
_____
_____
_____
_____
_____
_____
_____
_____
_____
_____

TOWARD AN EMBODIED, SENSUAL FAITH

"When spirituality and sexuality come together, we find our lost security"
—*Thomas Moore*

I recently traveled with a group of LDS couples through Andalucia, the southernmost region of Spain. Over the course of our eleven-day retreat, we explored the rich culture and historic towns of the region while learning how to create more intimate and soulful marriages. Our time together was filled with immersive cultural experiences such as tasting olive oil at a generations-old vineyard and crafting mosaic tiles under the guidance of a local artisan. Our retreats are designed to help couples deepen the intimacy and vitality of their relationships, and shared discovery often invigorates that connection. As couples step outside of their routines to explore new places, meet new people, and engage in unfamiliar activities, they often discover new dimensions of themselves and each other.

Beyond the increased intimacy of experiencing each other in novel ways, these activities offer couples the opportunity to *play* together—to tap into a vital, often-overlooked source of shared pleasure. Just as interpersonal growth breathes new life into a marriage (as explored in previous chapters), so too does simple *enjoyment* of one another.

215

Play, as shared physical enjoyment, invites the expansive energy of eros in a powerful way. Our bodies are remarkable in their ability to connect us, to create shared meaning through movement, laughter, and touch. Nowhere was this power more evident than during our final group activity, set in the vibrant city of Seville.

We had come to experience flamenco—a gritty, sensual dance form forged over centuries through the blending of diverse ethnic influences. Its development was catalyzed most by the arrival of the Roma people in Seville during the fifteenth century. Having served my mission in Seville, I returned to the region with my family a few years prior to this couples' tour.

During our stay, we took a walking tour of Triana, a working-class neighborhood once home to the Sevillan Roma. As we wandered the narrow streets, our guide pointed out the secluded courtyards typical of the area. He explained that the Roma lived as outcasts in white, Christian Spain. In the face of their exclusion and hardship, they would gather in these interior spaces to dance out their tribulations and find solace in their shared struggles. It was in these intimate, defiant gatherings that flamenco came to be the passionate, soulful artform that it is today. Even now, hundreds of years later, flamenco is still intimate, and best performed in small venues amid a responsive, engaged audience.

Naturally, learning flamenco was part of our couples' tour itinerary. Upon arriving in Seville, we met Cristina, an instructor at the Flamenco Dance Museum. Cristina introduced our group of mostly middle-aged and inexperienced dancers to the rhythmic footwork, expressive arm and finger movements, and the sharp, syncopated clapping so characteristic of flamenco. The experience was as fun as it was humbling, and we returned the next day to watch Cristina and the other dance instructors perform for us.

We gathered in a small courtyard framed by classic Andalusian arched porticos. In this intimate space, the first group of dancers assembled, drawing us in with their soulful rhythms and hypnotic movements. Then, as a mournful melody rippled from a lone guitarist, Cristina emerged onto the stage in a deep red, ruffled dress. Her presence was magnetic. She moved with a raw, almost primal energy—each motion controlled and exact—yet flowing with an effortless grace. We were captivated by her, and I felt as if my heart would burst as I took in the emotional intensity of her dance, moved by the sheer beauty and soul in it.

While in the emotion of the moment, Cristina turned to us, her students, and began to clap the familiar flamenco rhythm she had taught us the day before. We clapped for her in unison as she moved from an internal, dark energy to an expansive and determined one. Clapping in communal support of her, several of us inexplicably began to cry. The heartbreaking intensity of the experience was mysterious—I couldn't put into words why watching her was so moving. There was a rapture and transcendence in the room, an energetic communion between her and us. It was intimate. And in this moment, I felt visceral, inexplicable grief *and* joy—bittersweetness. My soul could feel it. When I attempted to recount this numinous experience to my husband and friends upon returning home, I would invariably tear up just in the recollection, unable to explain or even comprehend the emotionality and transcendence of it.

In my later research about flamenco dance, I discovered that we had experienced what the Spanish call *duende*—an intimate communication between the dancer, the audience, and God. Duende is a type of embodied communion or prayer, and for it to appear, there must be a particular chemistry between the dancer and the group. While I had seen flamenco performed many times before, I had never been moved so deeply or experienced so much emotion.

As I struggle now to put my experience into words, it is reassuring to read Spanish poet Federico García Lorca refer to duende as "a mysterious power that everyone senses but no philosopher can explain."[1] His insight speaks to the profound spiritual meaning that can be communicated through the body—a kind of knowing that speaks directly to the soul. As English poet William Blake observed, "the body is indeed the soul manifested by the senses."[2]

KNOWING THROUGH THE BODY

Socrates is said to have called the body an instrument of perception. It maps and communicates interpersonal meaning in ways that defy verbal and logical expression. The flamenco dancer's skillful, artistic movement communicated an ineffable apprehension of loss, human sorrow, and fierce resilience. Only later did I learn her performance was called "The Dance of Death." She had communicated to our souls meanings that words cannot adequately convey. As a student of mine said about her attempt to put a spiritual insight into words, "It was like trying to translate a perfectly pure language into sloppy human." Indeed, the body's spiritual power lies in its ability to comprehend and communicate meaning outside of "sloppy human." The verbalizing and linear mind is always trying to catch up.

Perhaps contrary to our intuitions about our physical selves, a body is essential to the soul because we perceive spiritual truths *through* it. One of my students, a choreographer, put it this way: "There have been times when the movement of my body felt holy, like I was tapping into something not actually mine—older than me, ancient—some kind of generational, perhaps eternal, somatic wisdom. I don't know how else to describe it." Similarly, Catholic theologian and psychotherapist Thomas Moore describes the spiritual power of the body this way: "The body is indeed a temple, not simply for its beauty and value, but because it houses the holy mystery of human existence."[3] The body doesn't obscure spiritual truth; it reveals it.

Our bodies are holy things, not obstacles to our spirituality, and not the definition of "natural man" that scripture characterizes as the enemy to God. As we have been learning, "natural man" is instead ego—self-preoccupation—and indeed natural because we all begin life in this egocentric state. This fact is not sinful in and of itself; rather, the sin lies in any choice to coddle our innate narcissism at the expense of our growth. Sinfulness lies in the demand that the world submit to our desires, fears, and self-importance.

In fact, King Benjamin makes no mention of lust or sexuality in his discourse in the Book of Mormon. Instead, he emphasizes that the sin of the "natural man" lies in our refusal to yield to the "enticings" of the Holy Spirit that invite us to grow beyond our egocentrism—beyond our limited selves. It is not the body, not the sensual, and not the material world that is contrary to the spiritual: it is pride and the refusal to repent. Indeed, we need the body to deepen our spiritual wisdom and to increase our capacity for joy.

SENSATION & SPIRITUALITY

In a faith culture that values "bearing testimony" and the confession of certainty, we often equate spiritual depth with unwavering confidence in our shared beliefs. The ego certainly prefers a spirituality focused on certitude and transactional agreements with God over a spirituality that asks us to love one another in our shared uncertainty and suffering. Why *wouldn't* we want control in a fallen world? Obeying the rules in exchange for security is a desire that certainly makes sense. Our impulse to find order and predictability in the midst of disorder and pain is both understandable and deeply human.

But as we endure life's inevitable losses, our spirituality tends to become a spirituality of recognition—a spirituality that perceives the beauty and wonder in life amid the necessary sorrows and hardships. And though our souls can feel a deep order within reality—divine truths we are all subject to—we understand that faith doesn't grant us certainty or obviate suffering. Rather, it offers us solace, evidence of God's love in sublime moments, and glimpses of the eternal that anchor us in a world full of loss.

Sacred and sublime moments like these are perhaps best characterized as *liminal,* a word meaning "threshold" or "in-between" that captures the essence of spiritual experiences. In moments of awe or wonder, we can feel suspended between heaven and earth—grounded in our lived experience and yet momentarily lifted beyond it.[4]

Anthropologist Victor Turner describes liminality as a "betwixt and between" state where the ego dissolves, and something more communal, spiritual, or sacred can emerge.

As spiritual beings, our souls seek the liminal. We are drawn to threshold experiences where the known and unknown meet. This is where our souls are nourished and sustained. Most religious traditions and practices invite us into liminal experience where the material and spiritual come together. Traditions and rituals root us in the here and now, while simultaneously opening us up to something beyond the tangible and visible. Recall the scene at the Jewish wedding when my husband and I danced the Hora around the jubilant couple. This exultant moment was both embodied *and* transcendent: grounded in the physicality of a centuries-old tradition, while drawing us into a suspended moment of shared meaning and joy.

These liminal moments not only offer our souls meaning and reassurance, they beckon us out of our egocentric orientation toward a wiser understanding of who we are and our proper relationship to one another. For example, when I was a student in Israel, I summited a peak in the Eilat Mountains. Wandering away from my hiking companions, I reclined on a wide stretch of rock. With the solid earth beneath me and an expanse of stars overhead, I found myself in this striking duality: anchored and elevated—fully rooted in the physical world while also transported beyond it.

In this numinous moment, I understood at once my insignificance and my significance—I was inconsequential in a vast universe, and yet, deeply connected to all of it. The experience invited me to mature. Because in holding both truths—that I was at once significant and nothing—I could see beyond my natural self-centeredness, and for a moment, I could see myself and others more compassionately and truthfully.

Again, sensation—the way we encounter the physical world—doesn't oppose the spiritual; it opens the door to it. The physical body gives us a path out of our anxieties and self-concern into the sublime. Taking in the brilliant colors and textures of the changing seasons or feeling the salty spray of crashing waves against the shore—these kinds of experiences readily inspire our sense of awe. Even quite ordinary encounters with the physical world can transport us for a moment—the scent of worn books lining a family bookshelf or the inhale of crisp air on an autumn morning. It is often in the most ordinary of sensations that we become attuned to something spiritual—the attunement to beauty accessible only through the body. The poet David Whyte describes it this way: "Beauty is an achieved state of deep attention and self-forgetting; the self-forgetting of seeing, hearing, smelling or touching that erases our separation, our distance, our fear."[5]

These moments of communion with the ordinary are a kind of grace—divine gifts available to us through the body that remind us of God's love. To fall in love with creation, to truly receive it with joy, is itself an act of worship—a way of offering praise to the Creator.[6]

223

When I brought a group of LDS couples from the Intermountain West to Florence—the birthplace of the Renaissance—we experienced firsthand the power of our senses to open us up to spiritual sustenance and joy. For many, our initial immersion into such a vividly sensual culture was disorienting. The ubiquitous celebration of the human form stood in striking contrast to our more conservative cultural norms and unspoken anxieties about the body. Some felt uneasy at first viewing Michelangelo's *David* and other Renaissance masterpieces. Was it acceptable to appreciate the naked form if it was found in a museum? Was this a kind of pornography?

Yet, surrounded as we were by Florentine sculpture and art over multiple days, the group's discomfort dissipated as they began to take in the physical beauty before them. In time, they recognized for themselves the wisdom in the Renaissance perspective—that the human form, far from being something to fear, is indeed God's masterpiece.

In Italy, sensual beauty permeates every facet of life—from the sublime art and sculpture to the graceful symmetry of its architecture; even the cuisine is an aesthetic endeavor. Italian culture is steeped in the epicurean belief that sensual pleasure is critical to our spiritual wellbeing, and we should cultivate the pleasures that soothe and uplift the soul. (Pleasure pursued solely for the sake of indulgence or hedonic thrill runs counter to epicurean ideals because it works against joy.)

Immersed in this epicurean way of life, the couples gradually opened themselves to the sensual beauty and pleasure that surrounded them. Instead of merely consuming food, they began to *savor* it. And rather than simply viewing a work of art, they began to fully *experience* it. The sensual world was drawing them out of their logical, cautious minds into the wisdom of the body. As they surrendered to it, they were becoming more attuned to the preciousness of their lives and the profound value of one another.

Upon returning home, several couples shared that their marriages felt stronger than ever. By opening to the beauty around them, they found a soulfulness that softened their hearts and deepened their gratitude. They were experiencing a kind of knowing beyond reason—an embodied wisdom found in receiving the pleasures of life and of each other. They were living what Nietzsche observed: "There is more wisdom in your body than in your deepest philosophy."[7]

Of course, we don't need to travel to Italy to access the wisdom and spirituality of the body. We can open ourselves to the sensual pleasures in the here and now—savoring the aesthetic delight in a well-prepared meal, taking in the soul-stirring sights and sounds of nature, and receiving the quiet peace in a loving touch. Yet, too often, we live in a hurried, hyper-productive state, convinced we must earn joy or pleasure—only after the to-do list is complete or our flaws are finally overcome. Many of us also fear that the sensual will corrupt our moral sense. But in our well-meaning austerity and resistance, we unwittingly alienate ourselves from our own souls and from one another.

Films like *Babette's Feast* and *The Taste of Things* explore the spirituality of receiving life's sensual and aesthetic richness. In *Babette's Feast*, for example, the religious characters initially resist pleasure of any kind, believing it will compromise their virtue and spiritual devotion. But as they open themselves to the sensuality in the meal set before them, they are quietly transformed. Their deep enjoyment draws them closer to each other and to divine grace. In daring to receive from a generous God, they discover true delight, and their souls are nourished by it.

We too can surrender to God's goodness offered to us in the physical world, taking time to savor the beauty and abundance in life. Such receptivity is an expression of faith—it reflects a trust in our own worthiness and in the goodness of God. When we receive with open hearts, our souls are nourished, and we awaken to the sheer wonder of being alive. Far from being an escape from life, this kind of surrender draws us more deeply into it—inviting a soulful communion with ourselves, with those we love, and with the Divine. It is in this spirit that we rejoice in the gifts God has placed in the world for our flourishing (see Doctrine & Covenants 59:18-20).

Much like the characters in *Babette's Feast*, the couples who traveled with me to Italy were awakening to the deep, life-giving energy of eros. As we explored in chapter I, eros lies at the heart of human thriving. The soul does not flourish in indifference or detachment; we are drawn instead to passion and pursuit. We are animated by a hunger for what we do not yet fully know—for what we have not yet experienced. In other words, eros is the human longing to become more than we are—to reach, to create, to be in communion with all that is beautiful, good, and true. It is the divine spark that awakens our spirit, the sacred yearning that draws us toward something more. Perhaps it is this spiritual longing that most defines what it means to be human.

Toward an Embodied, Sensual Faith

What often stands in the way of our willingness to enter the uncertainty of eros is the ego—our resistance to risk, our instinct to meet vulnerability with dominance and control. Of course, reason, skill, and the tools that improve our lives are essential. It is both right and necessary to use every resource at our disposal to ease our suffering. Yet no tool, no accomplishment, no form of control can ultimately shield us from the vulnerability of being alive. We must endure the uncertainty of living with agency in a fallen world. As the book of Ecclesiastes reminds us, all of our attempts to prevail over the fragility and vulnerability of existence, in the end, fall short.

227

Sooner or later, each of us faces illness and death, and we must endure separation from those we love, even if only for a time. Mortality ultimately shatters our illusions of control and forces us to confront the limits of our capacity. King Solomon grieved: "I did set my heart to seek and search out by wisdom concerning all that is done under heaven; this burdensome task God has given to the sons of man . . . I have seen all the works that are done under the sun; and indeed, all is vanity and grasping for the wind. What is crooked cannot be made straight, what is lacking cannot be numbered" (Ecclesiastes 1:13–15 NKJV). Our world is undeniably fallen—one where suffering is not the exception but our shared reality.

Our reflexive pursuit of invulnerability not only fails us, it denies the soul what it needs most. More than control, the soul longs for meaning and connection. No degree of certainty or mastery can satisfy the deeper need to know we are loved, and that we are capable of loving in return. As the French philosopher Jean-Luc Marion reminds us, it is only love—freely given and received—that truly sustains and assures us.[8]

After the death of my mother, my family and I found ourselves confronting the harshness of mortality. In our raw grief, my brother expressed something I was also feeling—that the only real power we have is in choosing to love each other. It is the only balm we have to offer, yet it is powerful. Love is what grants us both meaning and security;

it is the surest anchor in life's storms. And as the New Testament teaches us, love not only binds us to one another, it draws us into communion with God: "Beloved, let us love one another: for love is of God; and every one that loveth is born of God, and knoweth God. He that loveth not knoweth not God; for God is love." (1 John 4:7–9).

While love binds us to one another and the Divine, to love is to open ourselves to heartbreak. Intimate love requires vulnerability—it asks us to reveal our imperfections and lay ourselves bare. To desire another is to risk disappointment, exposure, and the ache of loss. As C.S. Lewis says, "To love at all is to be vulnerable. Love anything, and your heart will certainly be wrung and possibly broken."[9] Because love does not offer us guarantees. It sometimes leads us to joy and other times to heartbreak—most often, it leads us to both. Love requires the willingness to give ourselves without knowing what will come in return.

Loving, then, is an act of faith. It expresses our trust in love itself, in our own worthiness and in the reality of goodness. In my view, the courage to love—to reach beyond certainty and comfort towards others—is the most meaningful expression of faith in God. Our actions reveal what we value and what we will sacrifice for. To love God is to love others—and to love others is to let our souls be shaped by compassion, vulnerability, and grace.

"Once in a lifetime you look at a stranger and you see a soul."[10] In writing about eros, novelist Marilynne Robinson gives language to what I felt the moment I opened the door to find John standing on my front porch in Boston. He had come to visit my roommate, but after a brief exchange, I was unexpectedly and undeniably drawn to him. There was something both familiar and at the same time mysterious about him. I was experiencing the pull of eros—the quiet, inexplicable yearning for another soul.

When John and I began dating nearly a year later, the early intense attraction gradually softened to reveal gaps in our connection. The very same introversion that I found so alluring at first could also be isolating and unsettling for me. John was at times ruminative and reserved in a way that activated my insecurities. And after meeting his quiet and intellectual family, I wasn't sure I was equal to them or if I'd find acceptance there.

Deciding we were simply too different, I resolved to end the relationship and prayed for confirmation of my decision. But instead of a divine validation, I experienced a quiet, unsettling invitation to see John more truthfully. And in that brief, luminous moment, I perceived John's inherent goodness and the gift for me there if I was willing to grow into someone more loving—into someone more real.

Although this invitation touched something deep in me, I wanted to ignore it. I was uninterested in seeing clearly—uninterested in truly loving. The uncomfortable truth was that I was seeking something for myself in marriage. I wanted someone who would soothe my insecurities, someone outwardly impressive and affirming who would make me feel worthy by association. Uncertain that I would get the ego-reinforcement I craved with John, I turned away from this invitation and broke up with him anyway. I wasn't ready to open my eyes to the soul before me—the one I already knew could see me.

Yet, the more tightly I clung to fear and the illusion of control, the more my unhappiness grew. It wasn't until months later that I came to a more honest place within myself—one that made it possible to truly choose the relationship. In my wrestle, I began to face the depth of my own neediness. I recognized that I had been viewing John—and any imagined future partner—primarily through the lens of what he could be for me. I was also waking up to the fact that I used critique as a shield, as a way to justify receiving love without having to risk offering it. By leaning out of the relationship while John leaned in, I could extract temporary security and approval without offering my heart in return.

Despite my growing self-awareness, actually *choosing* John—stepping in with two feet—terrified me. To commit fully meant opening myself in ways that felt frightening and vulnerable. And to marry was to live within the constraints of our respective limitations, without an easy out when I felt unseen or when love asked more of me than I knew how to give. Yet, even knowing these risks, my soul wanted to become capable of loving another person, and John was the one I wanted to share my life with. Whatever invalidations and risks were a part of that choice, I wanted to be enough for them. With that hard-won clarity, I stepped into the unknown—making the erotic decision to choose John as fully as I knew how.

LOVE AS A CHOICE

As author Tamara says, **"To make an erotic decision is to be willing to lose the self you were, for the self that might be born in the act of choosing."**[11] When we first fall in love, we are immersed in eros—swept up in a rush of passion and affirmation that makes us feel vividly alive and offers us a taste of what a relationship can be. While this initial immersion is full of delight and wonder, *sustaining* eros in marriage asks far more of us. Once the proverbial honeymoon ends and our differences begin to surface, love becomes a matter of deliberate choice—an act of agency, an act of *self*.

For the aim of eros love is not to satisfy a need or fulfill an obligation. It is, instead, to offer the truest and deepest parts of ourselves to another. It is love freely given. It is to live in alignment with the soul's longing for connection rather than the ego's want of control. To live erotically, then, is to make choices that carry uncertainty and exposure, yet fill us with life. Such decisions break us open, but they lead us unfailingly to something stronger and something more worthy.

LOVE'S UNVEILING

Late one morning I sat with John in his kitchen as a soft veil of sunlight poured through the window, bathing the room in a quiet warmth. The possibility of marriage was in our thoughts and conversation. Looking at John across the table, I could see with a piercing clarity the kind and steady soul before me. Despite months of my own ambivalence and uncertainty, in this moment, a sense of wonder washed over me. I couldn't believe John's desire for me was real, and that he was choosing to share his life with me.

In choosing him fully, I had not only liberated myself and our relationship from my consternation and perfectionism, I could now see John as he truly was. I was experiencing what Jean-Luc Marion describes as the pure recognition of another soul—a moment of seeing the divine within another person and being moved by its beauty. "The lover makes appear the one whom she loves, not the reverse."[12] Erotic love is to behold our lover's soul and say, "I cherish so many things about you, but it is your mere existence that I love you for most."

233

Desire is a spiritual act. By this, I do not mean the anxious grasp at gratification or the attempt to take something for ourselves, but the soul's longing to transcend our insular reality and commune with the world. Desire is the faith that opens our hearts and draws us beyond ourselves—the sacred yearning to become more than we currently are.

In erotic desire, we are instinctively drawn to mystery: yang seeks yin, the masculine yearns for the feminine, the familiar reaches toward the unknown. There is always a threshold: a bridge to cross, a mystery to enter, new terrain to explore. The erotic beckons us into the transformative unknown.

Our attraction to difference in romantic love is central to the generative power of the erotic. The very polarities that spark desire draw us to our beloved even as they unsettle us. A spouse's opposing inclinations will likely appeal to us as much as they irritate. Yet it is precisely this tension that stretches us beyond ourselves—shaping us into people capable of truly loving another soul. This erotic tension is what keeps us awake to each other and passion alive. It is why struggle and bliss live side by side in any honest marriage—just as they do in sex. They are the contraries that transform us, the tensions that give birth to new life. And though we may at times resist or even resent the friction of honest partnership, it is precisely through these conflicts and tensions that something enduring and beautiful is forged.

SEX AS A SACRAMENTAL MEETING

*"The world is full of small wonders.
Sex can be one of them."*
—*Stephen Snyder*

Because the body communicates profound meaning, sexuality can be a powerful pathway into the sacred. Even as we descend into the depths of our physicality, we can experience one of the most elevating and unifying of human realities. Contrary to our common religious intuitions, we experience the sacred *in* the profane. We witness the eternal and spiritual through the impermanent and physical—just as Mircea Eliade observed.

Nowhere is this truth more evident than in intimate moments, when the language of the body (our mother tongue) reveals what words cannot. It is through the body that we first knew we were loved, through touch that we first experienced ourselves as a *self*. When intimate touch conveys full acceptance—when it expresses a spouse's genuine pleasure in our being—sex becomes a kind of coming home. Such embodied acceptance reconnects us not only to our earliest memories of love, but also to our truest selves. This is what we long for with an intimate partner: to know they are glad we

235

exist—that it is our soul they most desire, and that we are known and valued, exactly as we are. This is the animating meaning of good sex.

This grateful, intimate connection is what makes sex the sacrament of a marriage. Sex is its essential spiritual practice for its ability to reveal the sacred in the ordinary. In *The Soul of Sex*, Moore describes lovemaking as a vital marital ritual in its ability to draw us out of the routines of daily life into the restorative space of the erotic. Sex, he says, mediates between worlds, "between the daily concerns of living and the eternal concerns of meaning and the heart."[13]

Experiencing the sacred in sex does not depend on peak encounters. Even the simplest moments of honest connection can be sanctifying. By being fully present to an intimate moment—by *receiving* it—we "sanctify the ordinary," in Snyder's words. We open ourselves to the beauty and wonder woven into the ordinariness of our lives and love. Arousal lifts us out of the normal rhythm of time, transporting us into sublime moments where the world falls away and it feels as though we might go on forever this way. It is this fleeting brush with the eternal that gives sex its enduring hold on our hearts.

The capacity to suspend time and open us into deep presence with one another, is also what connects sex to joy. We experience joy whenever we take in the wonder of a moment. As Walt Whitman wrote, joy is "not in another place but this place . . . not for another hour, but this hour."[14] It is to let these ordinary and precious moments bless us by giving ourselves fully to them—because we never know how many more we'll be given.

WE ARE THAT WE MIGHT HAVE JOY

"Joy is the serious business of heaven."
—*C. S. Lewis*

We learn in 2 Nephi that living with faith increases our capacity for joy. This is not the faith of blind obedience or naïve hope; it is a faith rooted in courage. To exercise faith in a fallen world is to love when hatred feels justified; it is to follow our heart and conscience when fear urges our retreat. It is the courage to follow our soul's longing, even when that path requires the ego's undoing. Faith in God and in goodness itself is to yield to the refining process that will shape us into our truest selves.

Through this surrender, we become new creatures—souls more capable of love, souls more open to joy. "I will give you a new heart and put a new spirit in you; I will remove from you your heart of stone and give you a heart of flesh" (Ezekiel 36:26). It is this softened, awakened heart—grateful and generous—that is capable of intimate joy.

"To allow ourselves to be joyful is to have walked through the doorway of fear," David Whyte writes. To love fully is to open ourselves to the "vulnerability of happiness and the vulnerability of its imminent loss."[15] Joy lives in the courage to give ourselves over to these moments—to be so caught up in love, in gratitude, and in connection with others, that our fears and the burdens of ego fall away.

Joy is not only felt in the heart; it flows through the body as well—in the pleasure of dancing, of food, of song, and of touch. It is the joy of sex and sensuality, the deep pleasure of loving and being loved. It lives in the recognition that our lives, and the people we share them with, are gifts. And to cherish these gracious gifts—even in the face of inevitable loss—is to know joy.

THE GIFT OF FAITH

While marriage can be loving and joyful, it can also be deeply painful. An intimate relationship unveils us. And moments of disconnection and conflict can leave us questioning whether we chose the right person or if we are capable of the love a marriage requires. These heartbreaks and disillusionments can shake our faith in marriage, in ourselves, and even in love itself.

Yet our faith offers us the gift of perspective. We live in a fallen world by design, and our struggles are not signs of failure but part of the soul work we are here for. Marriage, in its ability to expose our hearts, will reshape our souls if we'll let it. But this growth requires our willingness to rise above our self-justifications and self-preoccupations. It requires our faith. This isn't just challenging work, it is sacred work. It is the process by which we become more whole.

As you have read this book and engaged with the self-reflection questions, I hope you've come to see more clearly the ways you do *not* love—the ways you've contributed to painful patterns in your marriage and other important relationships. What truths about yourself or your marriage have you been avoiding? What needs your attention for you to live in deeper alignment with your own soul?

The choices we make in these moments of reckoning are the truest test of faith. While many of us profess *belief*, faith is demonstrated not by what we say, but by what we *do*. To have faith, then, is to choose what is good over what feels good. It is to love even when it frightens us, to give even when it reveals us. It is to address what we know is ours to change. These are the self-defining choices that shape not only the happiness of our relationships but the meaning and trajectory of our lives.

To reach beyond our current capacity is always an act of love and the place where new life begins. As I often remind my students, "Eros lives at the edge of our capacity." I have witnessed this kind of spiritual rebirth in couples: as they face themselves and undergo a change of heart, their souls and their relationships are filled with life. Their countenances change as they experience newfound hope and greater joy together.

For a sexual relationship to be erotic, to be life-giving, it must be anchored in what is real. We cannot fake our way into intimate sex. It begins with the shared desire to create something honest and loving. It requires a mutual willingness to come together—body and soul—offering our whole selves and discovering one another again and again.

To open ourselves to this kind of intimate love requires our faith: faith that we are worthy of pleasure and care, faith in our lovability and our capacity to love. It asks for our courage—the courage to witness and be witnessed, to know and be known. Above all, it affirms our trust in a generous God who longs for us to know joy.

Our capacity for joy is inseparable from our exercise of courage. As one of my students beautifully put it, "To be witnessed, and to deeply witness another, is the heart of divinity. It seems so simple, but it takes so much courage." It is my prayer that we may all choose this loving courage—and bless our souls, our marriages, and the world through it.

Let me know that you are always present,
in every atom of my life.

Let my words be rooted in honesty
and my thoughts be lost in your light,

Help me to be aware of my selfishness,
but without undue shame or self-judgment.

Let me keep surrendering my self
until I am utterly transparent.

Unnamable God, my essence,
my origin, my life-blood, my home.

TRANSLATED BY STEPHEN MITCHELL

TEN LESSONS TOWARD A
CHILD'S SEXUAL INTEGRATION

*Children learn by an adult's
example, not by their words."*
—Carl Jung

Having explored over the last several chapters a
more expansive theological understanding of the
body, sexuality, and its relationship to spirituality,
I want to offer parents and teachers some fundamental concepts to encourage children's ultimate
acceptance and integration of their sexuality. Not
everyone is a parent, of course; but my hope is
that all readers will benefit from understanding
these principles, since virtually all of us teach and
influence youth in the church and in our extended
families. Our aim as mentors is to discourage the
indulgent sexual ethic of the larger culture, while
encouraging our kids to see the body, desire, and
sensuality as meaningful spiritual gifts and as over-
arching sources of good in their lives. To achieve
this balance, here are ten principles that can facilitate your children's peaceful and integrated relationship to their sexuality.

LESSON ONE: YOUR KIDS WILL INHERIT WHAT YOU BELIEVE ABOUT SEX.

Whether or not we want it to be true, we will have an outsized impact on our children's view of sex and pleasure, and how to be in relationship to both. It is also true that we teach less by what we say and more by what we do. So how we live as sexual beings—how we feel in our bodies, how we relate to a marriage partner—will be observed by our children, even if we try to hide it. We reveal our minds even when we don't intend to, and most often it's through our behavior. So, what do we do when a sexually explicit scene suddenly appears on the television screen we are sharing with a child? That's the moment that exposes more about our comfort with sexuality and our confidence in our child's ability to navigate these messages than any particular lesson we may teach. Teaching that "sex is a gift from God" will ring hollow if we don't genuinely believe it and live as though it's true. If we quietly harbor the belief that the body and sensuality are inherent threats to godliness, we will communicate that anxiety to our children. If we believe that sensuality necessarily undermines spirituality, then our children may understand any limits on sexuality as a rejection of the body. This will certainly interfere with their ability to build a peaceful relationship between sexuality and spirituality. In order to be valuable mentors, it is essential that we work with our own (often implicit) anxieties and beliefs around sex and the body.

Start by looking at any residual distrust you harbor about loving and being loved in the language of the body. Do you truly believe we can create joy and spiritual sustenance for the soul through our bodies? This exercise in introspection will be time well spent. Being able to genuinely affirm this theological perspective within yourself means that your child will likely also trust in the goodness of the body—and in the goodness of a God that wants us to know joy.

Such clarity on your part will even allow your children to relate to sexual self-restraint *before* marriage as a path which can facilitate greater joy and pleasure *within* marriage.

LESSON TWO: YOU WILL HAVE "THE TALK" MANY, MANY TIMES.

In addition to taking an honest look at your own beliefs and behavior around sex, you will have many conversations with your children about the physical facts of sex and the values you believe are most likely to create a peaceful relationship with sexuality. Because talking about the body and sex can be uncomfortable, it is important to have open, thoughtful conversations early on and establish yourself as a reliable resource for them.

As for the physical facts, we should teach our children the specifics about their bodies and sexual reproduction. Our toddlers should learn the names of their body parts, including sexual organs. Naming facilitates self-knowledge and self-acceptance. By the time our children are eight years old,

Lesson Two: You Will Have "The Talk" Many, Many Times

we should sit down and talk about the specifics of reproduction. It can be challenging to puncture the innocence of an unassuming child, who may be a little overwhelmed by the reality of intercourse. (And of course, parents should be sensitive to the specific needs of a child who may need more maturity before this talk or who may need a conversation sooner than age eight.) However, if they do not learn these specifics from you, they will learn them from peers or others who do not share your values. Additionally, talking to your kids early is an opportunity to establish yourself as a trusted resource. So, books with visuals created for teaching children can offer clarity as well as reduce anxiety for both parent and child. (I've offered a list of such books at the end of this book, see PG. 287.)

Additionally, before children enter adolescence, parents should prepare them for the physical changes and processes (such as menstruation and wet dreams) that will come with puberty. Because teaching sexuality is not easy, many parents neglect to take up even these most basic conversations. In a recent survey of 600 students at Brigham Young University, 58 percent said that their parents gave them "few or no messages about sex." And while some parents, albeit the minority, make the effort to instruct their children on important facts about reproduction and the body, teaching those physical facts is the most basic role we will fulfill in facilitating our children's sexual integration. It's telling that in the same BYU study, only 8 percent of students surveyed reported that their parents gave them positive and consistent messages regarding sex.[1]

As we discussed above, you will be teaching your values by how you live. But in addition, you will address your kids' needs by also articulating your values around sex. When you teach your child about the realities of intercourse and reproduction, for instance, you should also convey what you believe is the best context for sex. Many LDS parents teach that sex is an important way for grown-ups to communicate love and care, and that the commitment of marriage offers the context most conducive to soul-satisfying sex (as we'll discuss more in Lesson 7).

Besides offering your values around sex in sit-down conversations, your child will also benefit from you helping them parse the many messages they'll receive outside the home. They will be bombarded with competing views from popular media, peers, and church instruction. They need your thoughtful perspective to help them make sense of it all. Help them come to a coherent view for themselves from the divergent ideas they'll encounter. In practice, this might be as simple as spontaneous discussions about the implicit meanings in various situations.

Here are some examples of what these situations might be:

LISTENING TO A POP SONG: "What do you think about this singer's view of sex?"

WATCHING A MOVIE: "I'm not crazy about this movie, because it's trying to teach the idea that it's 'liberated' or 'cool' to have sex casually."

AT CHURCH: "The fear of losing your value in a future husband's eyes if you are sexual is a motivation I disagree with. Your choices should always be in support of your dignity and being true to yourself, not about earning a future husband's love."

In each of these situations, you are offering your perspective and encouraging your child to consider their own beliefs. These conversations are especially important in helping your kids learn to be critical consumers of the many ideas around them. This allows them to sort out their own minds and make wise choices for themselves around sex. Parents' willingness to normalize sex and be in an ongoing conversation about it has been linked to children establishing a healthier view of sex.

LESSON THREE: OUR CHILDREN'S BODIES BELONG TO THEM, & THEY ARE WORTH PROTECTING & RESPECTING.

A foundational concept for our kids is that their bodies and their capacity for pleasure are gifts from God *to them*—and that their bodies belong to them alone. It is important to emphasize that celebrating this gift is part of accepting themselves and acknowledging their value in God's eyes. This ability to receive the gift of embodiment is connected to our children's self-respect, to their ability to intuitively respect the autonomy and dignity of others, and to expect such respect in return. Because our bodies are so connected to our souls, they are worth protecting from casual sexual interactions with others.

Teaching children about bodily autonomy could begin with teaching about touch. Help them understand that others should respect their wishes around touch and that they should also not touch others when it's unwanted. For example, you can help reinforce their healthy intuition around boundaries by respecting your toddler's wishes, even if doing so offends an adoring visitor or relative. Allowing your child to refuse even affectionate touch is a powerful way of living the truth that their desires and body integrity matter. Around six years of age, your child's natural sense of modesty will emerge and along with it, the desire for more privacy. She may suddenly no longer be comfortable changing in front of you. Again, respecting these desires demonstrates that you value her dignity and autonomy.

Another way to teach your children that their bodies belong to them is to only touch them as an expression of affection and care—never as a way to manage your own loneliness, neediness, or anxiety. A parent I worked with believed his wife was under-attentive to him sexually. He used his sense of deprivation and loneliness to justify his entitlement with his children. He would pressure them (and his wife) for affection and guilt them if they wouldn't give him a hug. While done under the guise of love and affection, the extraction of physical affection from children in this way can be very damaging. We should never ask our children to accommodate needy, entitled, or otherwise unboundaried behavior.

LESSON FOUR: OUR BODIES OFFER US A POWERFUL WAY TO LOVE & BE LOVED.

Because our bodies are integrally connected to our spirits, because our bodies are part of our souls, to love and be loved through the body is a powerful way to communicate love. It is our mother-tongue—the first language in which we are told we are safe, cared for, and cherished. For our children to become capable of physical love, which is essential to married sexuality, they need to experience touch as a form of care. Children in abusive or psychologically unsafe situations instinctively avoid real connection with others. This can translate into limiting the intimacy of sex in adulthood. That doesn't mean not having sex, period; it just means being unable or unwilling to access deeper levels of connection through sex.

People who have experienced human connection as exploitative will readily mask their heart in sex, use others for sexual pleasure or acceptance, or reject sexual engagement altogether. However, if we love our young children abundantly, kiss and hold them affectionately (when they are willing), and continue to be demonstrative and affirming as they grow, they will become fluent in the love language of the body. This will help them to intuitively love through their sexuality as adults, a capacity vital to happiness and intimate communion in marriage.

LESSON FIVE: DESIRE & PLEASURE ARE WONDERFUL PARTS OF BEING HUMAN.

It is important for our kids to understand that sexual desire and pleasure are valuable aspects of being human, essential to reproduction, and essential to creating a joyful life. Not only is sexual desire critical for keeping the human race going, it is a driving force that helps us to grow and move toward psychological adulthood. Sexual desire pressures us away from the security of familial love into the expansive realities of intimate connection and marriage—hallmarks of adulthood.

And yet, adults too often avoid the topic entirely when talking to their kids about sex, perhaps especially in the church. Despite its centrality to the human experience, too many of us treat sexual desire as a threat to our souls—as Satan's pathway into our hearts. And in this fear, we make the instinctive but ill-advised choice to ignore the subject altogether.

If we want our children to integrate their sexuality and develop a healthy relationship to eroticism, we must address the fact of sexual desire directly. Doing so is the best way to help our kids understand and navigate their feelings wisely. Without self-awareness, we inadvertently choose reactively, and our feelings run us, rather than our feelings merely informing our choices. When young people can name and make sense of their desires, they are *more* able to choose thoughtfully in response to them. In fact, if we have frank conversations about desire, we can inoculate our children from being overwhelmed by their impulses on the one hand, or fearfully suppressing sexual feelings on the other.

What messages should we be giving our kids about arousal and desire? It is helpful to first teach our kids *why* we experience arousal (defined as embodied sexual feelings we may not choose) and desire (the longing to be close to or sexual with another). Kids need to understand that embodied feelings are not temptations of Satan designed to divide us from God. Instead, arousal and desire are God-given and essential to our purpose on the earth. Without sexual feelings, we would not be motivated to do the soul-stretching work of committing to a partner and rearing children. Expanding beyond ourselves in the creation of a marriage and family is driven by embodied desire and is core to our spiritual growth as God's children.

Teaching that pleasure is dangerous, or a gateway to self-destruction, is actually not in harmony with our revealed theology. Of course, the headlong pursuit of pleasure *can* be destructive. We can indulge our way into a psychological hell and destroy the truest gifts in life if we make hedonism our god. But the soul's pleasure is anchored in morality and is integral to the good life. Pleasure in life, including in loving sexuality, is essential to our happiness. So while we want our children to understand that what we do in response to desire matters, we also want them to know that desire and pleasure are in and of themselves gifts from a loving God.

LESSON SIX: HOW WE RESPOND TO DESIRE WILL LARGELY DEFINE OUR LIVES.

Now that we've established that arousal and pleasure are God-given, we can show our children that they have choices, and that what they choose in response to sexual feelings will determine whether or not they create realities that sustain their souls. To experience intimate *joy* in sex, we must learn to manage our impulses and direct them purposefully. (Again, not because the body is evil, but because the body is a powerful communicator of meaning.) The meanings we create through our choices deeply influence whether or not sex will sustain us and enrich our most important relationships. Our kids need to understand that they have the agency to fundamentally shape what their sexuality will mean in their lives.

Throughout childhood, we must facilitate our kids' self-awareness around arousal and desire. They will benefit from knowing they are active choosers in response to these natural feelings, and that they have three possible responses:

to be sexual with another person,

to be sexual with themselves,

or to channel that sexual energy (eros energy) towards other endeavors.

Understanding these choices and considering the implications of each will help our kids consciously shape their relationship to sexuality through their decisions.

OPTION 1: Being physical with another person—from holding hands to intercourse—is generally the most complicated of the options because it involves another soul. You don't have just your own feelings to consider but also the feelings and expectations of another. Ask your child to consider: Is your degree of physical involvement commensurate with the level of emotional connection and commitment in the relationship? Do both of you feel the same way about one another? Is one of you taking unfair advantage of the other's interest? Are you compromising your own values to earn another's approval? Emphasize that intimacy and reciprocity don't develop quickly, so early physical engagement may interfere with developing the emotional aspects that are essential to a good relationship.

You can assert standards or expectations here as well—the guardrails around your children's autonomy—such as no dating until age sixteen, and limits on time alone with a romantic partner. One mother gave her teenage daughters this guardrail: "Enjoy expressing affection for your boyfriends, but don't allow them to touch any area that underwear covers. And pay them the same respect." Rules such as these protect your children from more freedom than they can responsibly navigate. Just make sure that your rules benefit your child's growing self-regulation and self-control, and not simply your anxieties about their growing independence.

OPTION 2: To be sexual with oneself, in the face of sexual feelings, is another possibility for your child. As much as this option may be uncomfortable for us as parents, the fact is that self-touch is normal human behavior. Babies masturbate in utero, toddlers explore the sensations in their genitals, and 80 percent of all seventeen-year-old males and 58 percent of all seventeen-year-old females have masturbated.[2] Despite the statistical normalcy of self-touch, many of us have a tremendous amount of fear about masturbation.

Lesson Six: How We Respond to Desire Will Largely Define Our Lives

While most of us can tolerate the idea of toddlers innocently exploring what feels good, adolescent masturbation is much more intimidating to most parents. This is probably due in part to the emerging eroticism (sexual thinking) that occurs naturally in adolescence. Not surprisingly, many of us wish that our teenager could suppress all sexual thought and stay more childlike in their sexuality. But this desire reveals our own struggle with eroticism and the misguided belief that virtue is equivalent to sexual ignorance. While this is understandable given our cultural confusion between sexual desire and temptation, the better route is to teach our children to accept their sometimes unruly, yet God-given sexual feelings and to choose well with them.

Being able to delay gratification is a valuable capacity. The more our children develop it, the better their lives will be. Sacrificing what feels good in the moment for our higher aims is an important muscle to develop. However, if we overreact to masturbation, we can do serious damage to our children by generating in them unnecessary anxiety about their sexuality. Sexual shame drives repression and compulsivity—precisely what we do not want for our children.

We can encourage self-restraint without relating to masturbation as a dreadful sin. Latter-day Saint authors Linda and Richard Eyre recommend in their book *How to Talk to Your Child About Sex* that we normalize masturbation as something almost everyone experiments with. Self-stimulation can become a problem if it is habitual or compulsive, they advise; but it doesn't serve us to try to *not* think about sex. The Eyres recommend instead that we teach our children to welcome emerging sexual feelings and to think about how good it will be to share them someday with a beloved other. When they do masturbate, the Eyres advise, teach them to think about the loving sex they hope to create with the person they will someday marry.[3]

What I love about this advice is that it teaches moderation as well as a direction for sexual feelings to go. It affirms sexual desire and channels it in a pro-social, relational direction. It trains one's sexual blueprint to be an expression of love, commitment, and intimacy. As we'll talk about later, this deliberate focus prepares us for the intimacy of marriage far better than the versions of eroticism found in pornographic material.

OPTION 3: The third option available to our children is to channel their sexual energy toward non-sexual goals. Channeling sexual feeling is not the same as sexual repression. Repression is the shame-driven denial of sexual feelings and the deliberate attempt to snuff them out. Fear-driven efforts to repress sexual feelings will always interfere with sexual integration.

Consciously channeling sexual desire, on the other hand, acknowledges sexual thoughts and desires, but deliberately aims to choose what we value most in the face of our choices. This redirection is deliberate and desire-based—choosing options that create one's desired life, rather than indulging impulses that will undermine it. In reality, we redirect sexual energy all the time. When an attractive person enters a room, most of us deliberately channel our sexual energy away from the individual. We don't leer, touch, or make sexual comments. The redirection doesn't require denying feelings of attraction. It only requires choosing propriety and respect for the stranger over sexual gratification. In other words, to channel sexual feelings is to *bridle* them. Bridling your passions—like bridling a horse—allows us to direct sexual energy toward larger goals.

Channeled sexual energy can be life-giving. Sublimated feeling is the basis of creativity, ambition, and a heightened sense of aliveness. By way of illustration, when my son was thirteen years old, a new girl moved into his school. She was impressed to learn that he played the piano, and that he was learning a song she loved. She expressed her hope to hear him play sometime. Completely energized by this magnetic interaction and motivated to impress her, he came home and practiced piano from the afternoon into the evening! Entirely new levels of ambition and focus emerged from his channeled adolescent sexual energy.

So the message for our children is that channeling sexual energy will not only create a life they are proud of, it will also make them more capable of intimate sex. When we are capable of deliberateness and sexual self-control, we build a sexual self-confidence and trustworthiness that is both attractive and essential to creating a secure sexual bond with another. These earned capacities are worth the sacrifice of immediate gratification.

LESSON SEVEN: PORNOGRAPHY IS A PROBLEM THAT REQUIRES A THOUGHTFUL RESPONSE.

Since the dawn of the Internet, we have been navigating a new ecology of sex and relationships. A couple of generations ago, getting access to sexual material required some commitment. Today our kids have unprecedented access to the most graphic and diverse sexual content. It is now a question of *when* they will encounter pornography, not *if*. In talking to our children about their choices, it is important to speak directly about the reality of pornography and simulated sexual experiences available to them in the evolving world of AI.

Creators of graphic sexual content know how to exploit what our brains are wired to seek and enjoy. In this uncharted terrain of excess, we have not evolved sufficiently to successfully navigate this level of brain-intoxicating novelty. Much like the food industry exploits our hard-wired desire for sugar and fat, we have an industry that exploits our wiring for visual stimulation and novelty. Our challenge as parents is to help our kids forge a healthy relationship to sexuality even while immersed in an unhealthy environment.

One of the ways we might fail in this endeavor is when we condemn our child's natural curiosity about pornography and sexuality. A child's draw to nudity and sexual images is entirely normal, yet we tend to respond in ways that suggest otherwise. While the discovery of explicit material in your child's internet search history can be jarring, shaming or overreacting can drive a child's pursuit underground, making it unavailable to address or understand. Although it is normal to be drawn to sexual images, *habitual* viewing of such imagery is not healthy. It can create unrealistic expectations of what intimate sex looks like. And just as we understand that a diet of sweets and processed foods is detrimental to a child's health, we recognize that super-charged, non-relational sexual content undermines a child's capacity to understand and create committed, intimate sex with a spouse.

So how do we help our kids? It is important to make them aware of the unhealthy environment they are navigating, and why it can be difficult to succeed. You might make this idea understandable through the example of a health-conscious student navigating the tantalizing desserts in a cafeteria each day. The availability of the desserts triggers the brain's hard-wired draw to high-calorie food, and can easily override the student's goal to consume

262

only nutritious food. In other words, the environment itself makes success far more challenging than if the cafeteria served only healthy options. The internet is a similarly challenging environment. Pornography is ever-present and designed to highjack our sexual minds. So it is no wonder that it can distract us from our larger values and interfere with our sexual integration.

In addition to helping your children understand the environment they are navigating, help them understand why sexual experiences, even when disconnected from a relationship, can be compelling. The privacy of pornography makes sexual exploration feel relatively safe. With porn, you don't have to risk humiliation or rejection. Because our sexuality is such a sensitive part of us, the perceived freedom from social judgment can be appealing. And since sexual pleasure feels good, it can take us away from the difficulties of everyday life. So when someone is bored, curious, or stressed, it makes sense that the pleasure of sexual feelings through porn could be a compelling choice.

Despite the ways that porn can *feel* like a solution, porn exploits one of the best parts of life. Caving into this intoxicating draw with any regularity will work against our ultimate freedom and sexual happiness. Managing emotions by going to non-relational sex can create a self-regulation habit that interferes with creating an intimate marriage. When we haven't learned to be with ourselves and our own emotions, and when we've patterned sexual arousal in a non-intimate and self-referencing way, we will have limited capacity for erotic depth and emotional ease with a real partner.

Again, the problem is not sexual imagery itself. Sexual gaze in the right context is a wonderful part of eroticism, and as I've discussed earlier, can even be transcendent and spiritual. The problem with pornographic content is that it doesn't usually sustain our souls or allow us to develop the psychological muscles we need to create intimate sex with a beloved and committed partner.

The freedom from sexual judgment provided through porn is small potatoes compared to what AI will progressively offer to society. Some experts have even suggested that AI sexual experiences will become so lifelike that it will be difficult to distinguish them from human partners. This may be true; but there is one huge exception: Real sex partners don't reinforce and validate everything we desire. Real relationships ask things from us, most particularly that we grow up, that we grow out of our demand for reinforcement. And although it is understandable to want an invulnerable way to be sexual, shallow and artificial validation works against the development of self-control, self-confidence, and the capacity for genuine human intimacy.

We can help our children through conversations that alert them to the risks of such patterns of sexual engagement. We can be deliberate in creating a healthy culture in our home through expectations and rules, including what sources of information we make easily accessible to our children. Curating the environment of our homes is important; not because nudity is evil, or because sexuality and arousal are inherent sins, but because we want our kids to become capable of meaningful, soulful sex.

LESSON EIGHT: THE BEST SEX IS MARRIED SEX.

Despite stereotypes of lifeless and infrequent sex in marriage, the truth is that the best and most regular sex is enjoyed by married couples—couples who have made the deliberate choice to *limit* potential sexual partners. In fact, wedded couples report greater happiness, including more emotional and spiritual contentment and better sex as compared to their single, cohabiting, or divorced peers.[4]

This is especially true for women, who are generally happier in committed sexual relationships compared to more casual ones.[5] Not only are women more likely to experience orgasm in a committed partnership because of greater familiarity, they are also more likely to trust opening up to a partner they feel loves and is invested in them.[6]

Yet, despite women's preference for sex with commitment, we live in an era that gives girls the message that sexual license—sex without commitment—is the same thing as liberation from oppression. While it is true that many women have been limited and controlled by the idea that sexual

265

purity is essential to one's value, many females are encountering a new demand on their sexuality: They must now prove themselves, not through sexual purity, but through uncommitted sexual engagement. Freedom from commitment purports to look like freedom from oppression, but in reality, it can be another form of it—another version of submitting to male sexual expectations rather than being true to their own.

That's why it's important to talk to our kids about knowing their desires and values and being faithful to them in their intimate relationships—especially if they are vulnerable to pleasing others at their own expense. Being true to our honest selves is the only way to create enduring freedom and happiness in a relationship. Commitment, entered into freely, is the key to creating the life and sexual relationship most of us hope for—and we don't need to apologize for standing up for it.

Marriage also creates an important boundary that enables couples to work out their differences, share their core selves, and forge a meaningful sexual friendship. The mutual promise to limit sexual options not only increases safety and trust, but also pressures growth in a couple as they work to create mutuality. A faithful marriage can be experienced as a prison or as a deliberate choice—entrapment or a way to value one's partner and one's sexuality. Committed sexual love can elevate the meaning of sex in our lives. This is neither a function of repression nor a rejection of sex; rather, it's a way to celebrate sex and increase its positive power in our lives.

LESSON NINE: SEX IS INTEGRAL TO OUR SOULS.

We live in a culture that promotes the idea that sex is simply about bodily sensations and the mutual exchange of pleasure, and that psychologically healthy people do not repress this physical, biological urge. But this perspective denies the fact that despite its basis in our biology, sex is not *just* "biological." Sex is personal and core to our being. And what we do with it impacts our souls, for ill or for good.

Sex carries the power to create life and to deepen love. It allows us to form deep attachments with those we share our bodies with—to create an emotional and physical bond. It also permits us to create a family that is the physical creation and extension of a couple. So sex is powerful and creative, and this capacity is connected to something deep within us, to the very core of who we are.

The potency of sex to impact our souls is also evident in how damaging sexual exploitation is. Sexual violation is profoundly traumatic and is far more spiritually wounding than someone stealing our belongings or even doing us physical harm. It is also true that couples who attempt casual sexual relationships often struggle to keep the emotional aspects of sex from interfering with their non-committal pleasure. Even if we want sex to be impersonal, the release of oxytocin (sometimes referred to as the "love hormone") complicates that outcome.

So even if we try to ignore the deeply personal nature of sex, it reveals itself in its impact on our lives and our hearts.

Because sex is so foundational to our sense of who we are, our sexual choices invariably shape our view of ourselves and our view of the world. When we express the value of restraint in the cautions we offer our children, it is not out of a belief that sex is evil. Our cautions should instead communicate the value of safeguarding this powerful part of our humanity, which, when related to wisely, can create strong love relationships, strengthen our souls, and offer us a meaningful source of joy.

LESSON TEN: OUR GOAL IS TO FACILITATE OUR CHILDREN'S SEXUAL SELF-AUTHORSHIP.

Our goal as parents is to help our children become the authors of their sexuality—the architects and agents of their lives. We want our kids to ultimately grow into adults who are capable of intimate connection through sex. Many of us mistakenly think our real goal is to keep our kids from having sex before marriage—that if our son or daughter makes it to the altar as a virgin, no matter how much sexual anxiety or baggage they bring with them, we have succeeded at our job. Of course, a child's virginity may be a welcome byproduct of the approach I am recommending, but our ultimate goal must be larger than behavioral measures. Our objective is to facilitate our children's ability to accept their sexuality and have a loving, joyous, committed partnership.

To do this, we must help our kids grow into adults capable of self-authorship in the very challenging realm of sex. Self-authorship in sexuality is often more difficult given the pulls of hedonic pleasure (in STAGE 1) and the appeal of social and sexual validation (in STAGE 2). These more immediate reinforcements can interfere with the ultimate integration of our sexuality and our peaceful relationship to it (STAGE 3). The task of a parent is to shepherd our children's movement through the stages of sexual development toward the integration of their sexuality and the ability to love and be loved through it.

Remember, achieving sexual integration means accepting ourselves as sexual beings and living according to our highest values with our sexuality. The reality is that sexual integration—or *sexual integrity*—is essential for sexual intimacy. Without it, we cannot truly love through our sexuality. We may be able to experience the body's pleasures, want a spouse, or accommodate their desires; but to bring our whole heart—to love and know through the body—requires presence in our own skin. It requires that we fully *inhabit* our sexuality. It requires that we are not divided within ourselves.

So how do we facilitate our children's sexual integration? How can we empower them to experience peace in their own skin? Of course, our guidance will be different with a young child than with a teenager. But at every age, we must hold the long view of our child's ultimate capacity for loving, meaningful sexual expression. And with that end in mind, we must give our children both the *limits* and the *freedoms* suited to their developmental stage to work out their relationship to this sacred part of themselves. Our children need to know sensuality and pleasure (**STAGE 1**), learn to inhibit or limit pleasure when socially necessary (**STAGE 2**), and then ultimately become capable of sexual integration and agency (**STAGE 3**). This is the developmental path that provides our children with the greatest chance of creating a loving, fulfilling sexual relationship.

It's valuable to understand and to let your child know that they will grow into their sexuality over many decades. This means that they will learn to manage their impulses and feelings imperfectly as they grow into their capacity for intimate sexuality. Mistakes are a part of living life and sorting out who we are. They are a part of developing skills. No tennis player can learn the skill of a backhand volley, for example, without error being fundamental to that process. Likewise, it is important to teach our children that they can (and must!) learn from mistakes and repent (change course). Mistakes can have

270

a cost, especially in the sexual realm, but our kids can use those missteps to change, learn, and grow.

While this developmental process is normal, our kids may learn unhelpful lessons at church that promote excessive fear around sexual missteps. Some teachers emphasize losing God's love, or losing desirability through non-marital sexual behavior. For instance, clients and women in my dissertation research often referenced chastity object lessons that compared sexual behavior with the destruction of value (with analogies to chewed gum). Others were taught that nails driven through boards might be removed, but the holes would always remain. We really need to avoid these fear-based messages that negate the reality of repentance and God's abiding love for us and focus instead on teaching our children that repentance and change are fundamental to the gospel. We should reinforce that we as their parent will always love, accept, and support them. This understanding of mistakes, God's love, and our love will encourage our children to be honest and to seek support when they need it. It will also help them believe in a compassionate God and offer compassion to themselves and others as they grow in their ability to love and be loved.

As parents, we play a critical role in helping our kids recognize the sex-positive nature of our theology, and the blessing that such wisdom can bring into their lives. We can teach them that the spiritual embrace of the body elevates their souls; we can teach them that our God-given sexuality can be a remarkable source of joy and peace in their lives as they grow into their ability to accept themselves

and love another. As daunting as this role may seem to you as a parent, the fact that you care enough to be reading these pages and seeking to do right by your children is significant. Remember, our kids track the meaning behind our verbal messages. Genuinely caring about your children will give them the most important message they need: That they are precious and beloved—that you are glad they are here.

APPENDIX:
MAKING SENSE OF PORNOGRAPHY

Pornography by definition is any visual depiction intended to arouse sexual interest. This encompasses everything from subtle and suggestive portrayals of the erotic to the explicit and even grotesque. By this definition, even drawings or intimate photos exchanged between spouses qualify. So, not all erotic images are inherently harmful. Similarly, not all portrayals of the body are created with the intention to arouse. Classical Renaissance art, for example, is a celebration of the human form and not intended to titillate.

Even so, our inherited fear of sexuality has left many of us so sensitized to nudity that nearly *any* portrayal of the body is seen as provocative. When there is a lot of anxiety around sex, and the body is considered forbidden, something as innocent as an exposed shoulder can stir sexual feelings. The more we fear and repress sexuality, the more susceptible we are to being overwhelmed by it. In this way, avoidance and repression can actually heighten our erotic sensitivity, making it harder to relate to sexuality in a grounded and integrated way.

The paradox in sexuality is that the more we make something prohibited or private, the more we intensify its erotic charge. For instance, most doctors working with the body see it as functional, not sexual. Similarly, there is nothing less sexy than a nude beach, where mystery—an important element in sexual desire—is entirely absent. In other words, it's not the exposure of the body per se that's erotic, but the meaning behind the exposure. Erotic charge is its highest when intimate exposure is not expected or allowed.

A non-LDS client of mine, doing humanitarian work in the Middle East, had an experience that exemplifies this well. Over several weeks, he worked alongside a Muslim woman. Both single, they gradually formed a deep attachment. As their time together came to a close and he was preparing to return to the United States, she removed her head covering when they were alone together. He told me that this moment was intensely erotic. As a Westerner, he had seen a lot of women's hair without much sexual meaning. But her hair, *this* hair, was private and personal, and her choice to share what was previously off limits carried an erotic charge.

In this way, a meaningful distinction between what is private and public can actually enhance erotic energy—especially when that boundary between what you share and what you keep personal arises from self-respect rather than repression and the fear of intimacy.

But when eroticism is cast as inherently dangerous—a slippery slope to spiritual failure—our fear-based approach usually backfires, leading to secrecy, shame and even obsession. In fact, some research suggests that people in more religious communities—such as the Bible Belt—are more likely to seek out online porn than those living in regions with less religious prohibition.[1]

The truth is, we are wired to notice the sexual. This desire is part of our survival as a species. And because the erotic thrives in mystery and the unknown, we are especially attuned to what is hidden—even what is prohibited. The porn industry exploits this human tendency. It makes easily accessible what has, for millennia, required investment in a person and a relationship. To keep people interested, the industry must continually escalate, offering increasingly exaggerated portrayals of the sexual—taking advantage of our desire for novelty and the allure of the forbidden.

This is not unlike our draw to junk food. Fat and sugar are essential to our survival, especially in times of scarcity. But in excess, they become unhealthy, undermining both our wellbeing and our ability to appreciate the pleasures of nutritious food. The food industry profits by designing products that exploit our biological impulses. And while it is understandable that we are drawn to junk food, its overabundance interferes with our ability to cultivate a healthy relationship to food and its genuine pleasures.

The pornography industry operates similarly. Not only can it distort our understanding of reality and what real sexual relationships look like, it can

275

also interfere with our ability to engage meaning-fully with others. At the very least, it offers an easier, less exposed way to be sexual—one that bypasses the relational challenges, growth and emotional exposure required of an intimate relationship. It can distract us from the pressures that would shape us into someone capable of real connection with another person—someone who will inevitably challenge and invalidate us.

Although pornography can interfere with a healthy relationship to our eroticism and to an intimate partner, not all arousal—or the sexual gaze that might invite it—is morally corrupt or harmful. Often, our discomfort stems more from fear of eroticism, rigid religious expectations, or unease with human sexuality itself. Ironically, a fear-based stance toward sexuality can result in sexual obsession—particularly in religious individuals—producing precisely the outcome we want to avoid.

THE COST OF OUR CULTURAL MISCONCEPTIONS

While some individuals genuinely struggle with compulsive pornography use, we should be cautious about pathologizing every encounter with it. Many religious individuals are quick to self-identify as addicts simply because they feel shame for their draw to sexual material. Research conducted at Brigham Young University showed that religious individuals are far more likely to label themselves as porn addicts, even when their behavior does not meet clinical criteria. Not only do they over-pathologize occasional use, the label of "addict" itself is associated with greater shame and relationship distress.[2]

As Dallin H. Oaks spoke about in a 2005 general conference address, it is important to distinguish between natural curiosity, periodic engagement, and compulsive behavior.[3] To over-pathologize any sexual curiosity or exploration can undermine our ability to understand our behavior and make conscious choices around it. It also fosters unnecessary and unhelpful self-loathing.

In addition, the philosophical framing of addiction often carries assumptions not only about the origin of the behavior but also its treatment. Many addiction treatment programs—modeled after substance abuse interventions—teach that the behavior lies outside of the individual's control. These models often reflect an implicit fear of sexuality itself and of its perceived power over the individual. Paradoxically, this approach can deepen feelings of powerlessness and increase anxiety around sex and desire.

It's important to remember that our goal is not to suppress desire, but to develop deeper self-regulation and integrity in our sexual choices. Programs that frame sexual feelings as inherently threatening only worsen the issue. When individuals are convinced they are out of control, they often become more obsessed, avoidant, and incapable of intimate connection with a partner.☞

Culturally, we often hear messages that "porn kills love"—that pornography destroys marriages and even souls. Porn use does indeed correlate with relationship distress, sexual anxiety, loneliness, poor self-esteem, and infidelity. But while these associations are real, current research does not confirm that porn causes these outcomes. In fact, many of these negative realties—social isolation, marital conflict, low self-confidence, and a tendency towards secrecy—can each be reasons for turning to pornography in the first place. In other words, porn use may well be an indicator of underlying distress as much as it is the cause of it. Even if pornography disappeared tomorrow, marriages would not automatically improve or become more intimate. Without a commitment to confront one's life and relationships with more courage and honesty, the avoidant or anxious partner may

☞ *Confessions of an LDS Sex Researcher: Faith, Sexuality, Science & Diversity* (BCC Press, 2024) is a valuable resource for anyone seeking to better understand a conflicted relationship with pornography. Drawing from his experience in faith communities, academic research, and clinical practice, Dr. Cameron Staley challenges the prevailing "porn addiction" narrative. Instead, he presents a nuanced view of pornography use—framing it not as addiction, but often as a response to emotional dysregulation and internal conflict. Staley offers a compassionate, science-based alternative that invites greater self-awareness and supports healthier, more integrated ways of relating to our sexuality.

simply find other ways to escape the challenges of marriage and intimacy.

While the evidence currently supports a correlation between pornography use and marital distress more than a direct causal link, this does not mean pornography is neutral or harmless. We need more research to understand what impact chronic porn viewing has on sexual development and behavior. But at the very least, our vices often serve as ways to avoid the soul work required of us—the hard work of honest and vulnerable engagement with life and love. Whenever we opt for an easy escape from the challenges of living in the real world and loving in real relationships, we weaken our self-respect, diminish our inner peace, and strain our relationships.

THE PATH TO SEXUAL INTEGRATION

It's important to recognize that not all erotic gaze is objectifying or reductive of another's humanity. There is a meaningful difference between a gaze that exploits, and one that affirms the beauty and desirability of a spouse. A sexual gaze can degrade— or it can express deep appreciation for the soul-beauty of another.

The longing for beauty is deeply human. As William Blake wrote, "The body is the soul perceived by the senses." Erotic beauty can be a window into the soul. To perceive that beauty through the body—through sexuality—is one way

279

we experience the sacredness of another. To be seen and desired without being diminished is deeply validating. It is soulful—and part of what makes intimate sex sacred.

Understanding our draw to the erotic as a longing for connection and intimacy can help us make peace with our sexuality. It can keep us from pathologizing desire as inherently sinful or self-serving.

As discussed throughout this book, being endlessly fascinated by sex—or endlessly afraid of it—are both distortions that cause suffering. Neither reflects spiritual maturity. Maturity requires cultivating an honest and respectful relationship with our sexual nature—acknowledging arousal, sexual curiosity, and the meaning these experiences hold for us. Erotic feelings are not always about love and commitment. While this can be unsettling, we must be willing to understand even our uncomfortable desires. Without self-awareness, we can't make conscious, values-driven choices.

For those who use pornography despite believing it is wrong, approaches grounded in self-awareness and self-authorship are often more helpful than those based in restriction and fear. Acceptance and Commitment Therapy (ACT), is particularly effective in helping people understand their motivations—including the disowned or uncomfortable parts of who they are—and move toward choices they can respect and stand behind with integrity.

When we are engaging in conflicted porn use (or any vice), it can be valuable to consider: *What am I getting from this behavior? What does it offer me? What would I lose if I were to stop?* Many clients insist they do not want to view pornography yet feel powerless to stop. While the dissonance between beliefs and behaviors can be distressing, it is often most productive to understand the part of you that does want to view it—and why.

Though facing these parts of ourselves can be uncomfortable, until our motivations and desires become clear—even the ones we'd rather deny—we remain vulnerable to them. The disowned parts of ourselves often hold the most power over our choices. Greater agency begins with greater self-awareness. And integration—not denial—of our lesser impulses is what gives us the ability to choose with intention and integrity. It puts us back in the driver's seat of our lives.

Ultimately, our goal is sexual integrity: to live in alignment with our values, honoring the erotic without being ruled by it. Moving toward that integrity requires curiosity over fear. What is your relationship with eroticism revealing—about your connection to yourself, to an intimate partner, to being known? Your sexuality doesn't need to dominate your life to be meaningful. And rejecting it won't bring you peace either. But living in deeper honesty—about who you are, what you long for, and how you love—is the path to greater integration, peace, and spiritual wholeness.

Scan the QR code for more of Dr. Finlayson-Fife's resources on understanding and addressing pornography use.

ACKNOWLEDGMENTS

My heartfelt thanks to Jana Riess, whose editorial insight and guidance on the first draft helped shape the foundation of this book. Her brilliant feedback was invaluable.

Thank you also to Lori Forsyth whose editorial input and support carried through to the final revisions. Her gift with language and her sound perspective were tremendously helpful.

To the friends of Faith Matters who generously read early drafts and shared their insights, and to Blaine Bassett and Spencer Phillips who offered meticulous edits of several chapters—thank you. You have all helped make this a better book.

To my talented assistant, Kristi Bassett—your gift with language helped me find the right voice when my words felt too cumbersome. Still greater has been your steady encouragement and unwavering support. I am deeply grateful for your friendship and generous heart.

Finally, thank you to the clients whose stories fill these pages. Your experiences and courage have deepened my understanding of faith, growth, and joy—and I am grateful.

ENDNOTES

INTRODUCTION

1. Jeffrey R. Holland, "of Souls, Symbols, and Sacraments," Brigham Young University devotional, January 12, 1988.

I

1. Robert J. Waldinger and Marc Schulz, Harvard Study of Adult Development, 2003.

2. Menelaos Apostolou, Christoforos Chritsoforou, and Timo Juhani Lajunen, "What Are Romantic Relationships Good For? An Explorative Analysis of the Perceived Benefits of Being in a Relationship," *Evolutionary Psychology* 21, no. 4 (2023).

3. Spencer W. Kimball, "Marriage and Divorce," Brigham Young University devotional, September 7, 1976; Ata Shakerian, Ali-Mohammad Nazari, Mohsen Masoomi, Painaz Ebrahimi, and Saba Danai, "Inspecting the Relationship Between Sexual Satisfaction and Marital Problems of Divorce-Asking Women in Sanandaj City Family Courts, Procedia," *Social and Behavioral Sciences* 114 (2014): 327–33; Haeyoung Gideon Park et al., "Sexual Satisfaction Predicts Future Changes in Relationship Satisfaction and Sexual Frequency: New Insights From Within-Person Associations Over Time," *Personality Science* 4, no. 1 (October 2023); Anthony Smith et al., "Sexual and Relationship Satisfaction Among Heterosexual Men and Women: The Importance of Desired Frequency of Sex," *Journal of Sex & Marital Therapy* 37, no. 2 (2011): 104–15.

4. Nicole Schmidt, "9 Surprising Health Benefits of Sex," WebMD, August 13, 2024.

5. Giovanbattista Andreoli, Chiara Rafanelli, Paola Gremigni, Stefan G. Hofmann, and Giulia Casu, "Positive Sexuality, Relationship Satisfaction, and Health: A Network Analysis," *Frontiers in Psychology* 15 (2024).

6. Haeyoung G. Park et al., "Sexual Satisfaction Predicts Future Changes in Relationship Satisfaction and Sexual Frequency: New Insights from Within-Person Associations Over Time," *Personality Science* 4, no. 1 (October 2023).

7. Kimberly Panganiban, "Fondness, Admiration, and Intimacy," The Gottman Institute, last updated May 15, 2025.

8. Parley P. Pratt, *A Voice of Warning and Instruction to All People, or, An Introduction to the Faith and Doctrine of the Church of Jesus Christ of Latter-day Saints*, 11th ed. (Deseret News, 1881).

9. James E. Talmage, in Conference Report, October 1913, 117.

10. Adam S. Miller, *Letters to a Young Mormon*, rev. ed. (Maxwell Institute, 2014), 53–60.

2

1. Richard G. Scott, "The Joy of Living the Great Plan of Happiness," *Ensign*, October 1996, 73–75. (Emphasis Added).

2. Russell M. Nelson, "A Plea to My Sisters," *Ensign*, October 2015, 95–97.

3. "Elizabeth Smart Discusses Purity Culture, Feminism in Online Interview," *Salt Lake Tribune*, September 24, 2016.

4. Christina Capatides, "A Cup Full of Spit, a Chewed Up Piece of Gum. These Are the Metaphors Used to Teach Kids About Sex," CBS News, April 29, 2019.

##

1. Robert Kegan, *The Evolving Self: Problem and Process in Human Development* (Harvard University Press, 1983), 266.

2. Richard G. Tedeschi, Jane Shakespeare-Finch, Kanako Taku, and Lawrence G. Calhoun, *Posttraumatic Growth: Theory, Research and Applications* (Routledge, 2018).

3. Kegan, *Evolving Self*, 41.

4. "Appendix 1: First Theological Lecture on Faith, Circa January–May 1835," The Joseph Smith Papers.

5. Marybeth Raynes, "How Sex and Spirit Are Linked: A Developmental Perspective," *Sunstone*, November 2001, 46–64.

7

1. Howard W. Hunter, "Being a Righteous Husband and Father, *Ensign*, November 1994, 49–51.

2. "Do What Is Right," *Hymns of The Church of Jesus Christ of Latter-day Saints* (1985), no. 237.

1. C. S. Lewis, *The Four Loves* (HarperOne, 2017), 123.

2. Lewis, *Four Loves*, 99.

3. Thomas Moore, *Care of the Soul: A Guide for Cultivating Depth and Sacredness in Everyday Life* (HarperCollins, 1992).

1. Federico García Lorca, *In Search of Duende*, trans. Christopher Maurer (New Directions, 1998). This quote appears in the essay "Play and Theory of the Duende."

2. William Blake, *The Marriage of Heaven and Hell* (1790).

3. Thomas Moore, *The Soul of Sex: Cultivating Life as an Act of Love* (HarperCollins, 1999), 91.

4. Moore, *Soul of Sex*.

5. David Whyte, *Consolations: The Solace, Nourishment and Underlying Meaning of Everyday Words* (Many Rivers Press, 2020).

6. Terryl Givens, "The Beauty of Communion: Love as Creative Force," *Wayfare*, Fall 2024, 179–81.

7. Friedrich Nietzsche, *Thus Spoke Zarathustra: A Book for Everyone and No One* (Penguin Classics, 1961).

8. Jean-Luc Marion, *The Erotic Phenomenon* (University of Chicago Press, 2006).

9. Lewis, *Four Loves*, 126.

10. Marilynne Robinson, *Jack* (Farrar, Straus, and Giroux, 2020).

11. Tamara, "Erotic Decisions: Desire, Disobedience and the Art of Becoming," Museguided, updated May 10, 2025.

12. Marion, *Erotic Phenomenon*, 80.

13. Moore, *Soul of Sex*, 203.

14. Walt Whitman, "Song of the Open Road," in *Leaves of Grass* (1856).

15. David Whyte, *Consolations: The Solace, Nourishment and Underlying Meaning of Everyday Words* (Many Rivers Press, 2015), 144–45.

10

1. Laura M. Padilla Walker research (BYU School of Family Life professor), 2017.

2. Cynthia L. Robbins, Vanessa Schick, and Michael Reece, "Prevalence, Frequency, and Associations of Masturbation with Partnered Sexual Behaviors Among US Adolescents," *JAMA Pediatrics* 165, no. 12 (2011).

3. Linda Eyre and Richard Eyre, *How to Talk to Your Child About Sex: It's Best to Start Early, but It's Never Too Late—A Step-by-Step Guide for Every Age* (Golden Books, 1999).

4. "About the National Survey of Sexual Health and Behavior," Indiana University Bloomington; Linda and Charlie Bloom, "Want More and Better Sex? Get Married and Stay Married," *Huffpost*, July 13, 2017.

5. Paula England and Jonathan Bearak, "The Sexual Double Standard and Gender Differences in Attitudes Toward Casual Sex Among US University Students," *Demographic Research* 30, no. 46 (2014): 1331.

6. "In Hookups, Inequality Still Reigns," *New York Times*, November 11, 2013, D1.

APPENDIX

1. Andrew L. Whitehead and Samuel L. Perry, "Unbuckling the Bible Belt: A State-Level Analysis of Religious Factors and Google Searches for Porn," *Journal for the Scientific Study of Religion* 57, no. 1 (2018): 80–95.

2. Nathan D. Leonhardt, Brian J. Willoughby, and Bonnie Young-Petersen, "Damaged Goods: Perception of Pornography Addiction as a Mediator Between Religiosity and Relationship Anxiety Surrounding Pornography Use," *The Journal of Sex Research* 55, no. 3 (2018): 357–68.

3. Dallin H. Oaks, "Pornography," *Ensign,* April 2005, 87–90.

FURTHER READING

While the endnotes provide many sources for research on specific topics, here are a few books of general interest I often recommend:

Love Worth Making by Dr. Stephen Snyder

Intimacy and Desire by Dr. David Schnarch

The Soul of Sex by Thomas Moore

The Four Loves by C.S. Lewis

For conversations with children:

It's NOT the Stork: A book about girls, boys, babies, bodies, families, and friends by Robbie H. Harris

The Care and *Keeping of You*, two books by Cara Natterson, one for younger and one for older girls

Guy Stuff: The Body Book for Boys by Cara Natterson

COLOPHON

The book title, chapter names, section titles, and page numbers are typeset in the type foundry Bitstream's cut of Lydian, a calligraphic humanist sans-serif typeface designed by Warren Chappell in 1938 and named for his wife, Lydia. His typeface is a masterstroke in expressing the elegance of pen-written strokes within a sans-serif skeleton. The text of the book is typeset in William, a modern interpretation of William Caslon's historic typeface, crafted by Maria Doreuli to honor tradition while meeting the demands of contemporary design. The footnotes and in-text endnote indicators are typeset in Freight Sans, designed by Joshua Darden.

The paper in this book is of archival quality and acid-free, produced from sustainable plantations.

Cover artwork by Colby A. Sanford.

Book design & typography by
Cole Melanson at TopoGraphic Studio.

AUTHOR

Jennifer Finlayson-Fife is a therapist, educator, and coach with a doctorate in Counseling Psychology. For over two decades, she has helped individuals and couples—particularly within the LDS community—strengthen their relationships and develop a more integrated view of sexuality. Through her acclaimed online courses, live workshops, and widely followed *Room for Two* podcast, she has supported the emotional and sexual development of thousands. Known for her clarity, compassion, depth, and humor, Dr. Finlayson-Fife is a sought-after voice on the topics of faith, intimate relationships, and personal growth.

 Learn more about Dr. Finlayson-Fife's online courses and other resources by scanning the QR code.